Designer: Malcolm Smythe
Editor: Catherine Bradley
Researcher: Cecilia Weston-Baker

Illustrated by Camel Pictures

Front cover: Portuguese soldiers advance cautiously through an Angolan village, suspected of being a guerrilla base, June 1972.

Designed and produced by
Aladdin Books Ltd
70 Old Compton Street
London W1V 5PA

First published in the United States in 1987 by
Franklin Watts
387 Park Avenue South
New York, NY 10016

ISBN 0-531-10319-6

Library of Congress Catalog
Card Number: 87-50226

Printed in Belgium

CONFLICT IN THE 20th CENTURY

AFRICA

FROM 1945

DR SIMON BAYNHAM
Edited by Dr John Pimlott

FRANKLIN WATTS

New York · London · Toronto · Sydney

INTRODUCTION

The continent of Africa, containing some 50 countries of widely differing political, ethnic and economic composition, faces substantial problems. Many of these have arisen as a result of European colonialism in the late 19th century. The arbitrary imposition of foreign rule created artificial territorial boundaries in areas historically divided along tribal lines. Political and economic patterns of life were introduced that meant little to the local people and led to opposition. During and after the Second World War, there was a rapid growth in demands for independence. When this was granted, the new countries were left with traditions which bore little relevance to the difficulties they encountered.

But it would be wrong to view Africa's problems purely in terms of colonialism. Conflict existed before the Europeans arrived, and tribal or ethnic differences still produce tensions which have nothing to do with a history of alien occupation. At the same time, Africa suffers many of the developmental problems which have come to epitomize the difficulties of the Third World. A large growth in population, coupled with the existence of ineffective governments, has in many cases put enormous pressure on traditional patterns of agriculture, leading to poverty and debt. Military coups, sometimes the only alternative to complete social collapse, have bred countercoups, armed opposition and even civil war, creating a spiral of violence which is often difficult to break.

These and other conflicts are likely to continue well into the 21st century. It is true that there are signs of a reduction in tensions in some parts of the continent but in other areas the prospects for peace seem grim. One such region is the southern Africa subcontinent where opposition to South Africa's apartheid policies has grown. Elsewhere civil uprisings have been prolonged by the intervention of outside powers in support of governments and guerrillas. But growing global awareness of Africa's problems, together with a realization that aid and technology must be channeled toward encouraging "self-help" among the African people themselves, may ease the economic difficulties that underlie much of the continent's political conflict.

DR JOHN PIMLOTT *Series Editor*

EDITORIAL PANEL

Series Editor:
Dr John Pimlott, Senior Lecturer in the Department of War Studies and International Affairs, RMA Sandhurst, UK

Editorial Advisory Panel:
Brigadier General James L Collins Jr, US Army Chief of Military History 1970–82

General Sir John Hackett, former Commander-in-Chief of the British Army of the Rhine and Principal of King's College, London, UK

Ian Hogg, retired Master Gunner of the Artillery, British Army, and editor of *Jane's Infantry Weapons*

John Keegan, former Senior Lecturer in the Department of War Studies and International Affairs, RMA Sandhurst, now Defense Correspondent, *Daily Telegraph*, UK

Professor Laurence Martin, Vice-Chancellor of the University of Newcastle-upon-Tyne, UK

The Author:
Dr Simon Baynham is Lecturer in the Department of Defense and International Affairs, RMA Sandhurst. He is the author of many publications on post-1945 Africa including *Military Power and Politics in Black Africa*.

Child soldiers in Angola: Portugal's withdrawal from Angola on November 11, 1975 saw the continuation of civil war among three rival claimants to government. The post-independence internal war entered its 12th year in 1987. As in Uganda, recruitment into uniform has not been limited to adults. Many children have been sucked into the conflicting armies' ranks.

CONTENTS

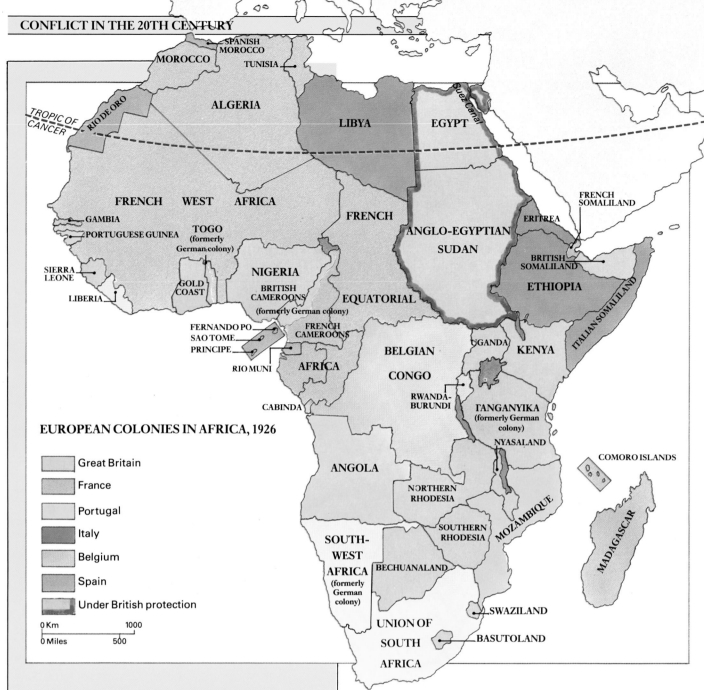

EUROPEAN COLONIES IN AFRICA, 1926

- Great Britain
- France
- Portugal
- Italy
- Belgium
- Spain
- Under British protection

0 Km — 1000
0 Miles — 500

CHAPTER 1
THE PARTITION OF AFRICA

Until the 1880s, European powers showed little interest in taking control of the territory of Africa, confining their presence to coastal areas and displaying deep ignorance of the interior. Within less than 20 years, however, the continent had been divided, often arbitrarily, among seven European colonial powers. Violent opposition was encountered, but by 1918, colonial rule had been firmly established.

By 1893 most of Africa and more than 100 million Africans had come under European rule. Yet in the mid-19th century, maps of Africa in school atlases portrayed it as a continent of blank spaces. The main geographical features – rivers, deserts, lakes, forests and mountains – were gradually filled in by the endeavors of British, French and German explorers.

In fact, Africa's enormous landmass (22 per cent of the world's total, greater than Asia and second in size only to the combined Americas) encompasses a rich diversity of peoples, cultures, climates and resources.

The discovery of human remains in Kenya suggests that the origins of man lie in Africa rather than elsewhere. From there the immediate ancestors of *homo sapiens* (thinking man) evolved and migrated throughout the continent and beyond. In 1900 its 30 million square km (11.6 million square miles) – completely surrounded by water except for a slender piece of land linking it to Asia – supported a population of 105 million. Today that figure has reached 500 million, double the number for 1960.

African peoples

Linguistically, Africa is one of the most complex regions of the world, with a total of around 1,000 indigenous tongues, some localized, some dialects of a group of languages. Several states use a major local language (for example, Swahili in Tanzania) officially alongside the former colonial one (usually English, French or Portuguese). Some 1,200 societies or ethnic groups have also been identified.

These range from primitive hunter-gatherers with a stone-age lifestyle like the Pygmies of the Congo and the Bushmen of the Kalahari Desert, to more sophisticated ethnic groupings like the Ashanti of Ghana and the Hausa of Nigeria. These differences are paralleled by distinct cultural patterns relating to dress, custom, myths of origin and religion. North of the Tropic of Cancer, most Africans are Arab believers in Islam; below this line, the majority of the population are Christian or believers in traditional religions.

Geography and resources

The Sahara Desert, 2,400 km (1,500 miles) across, spans the northern width of Africa. It divides the continent and represents something of a barrier. Unlike those countries with Mediterranean coastlines, most of the territory south of the desert has developed undisturbed by outside influence. In relief, Africa is a vast plateau surface with narrow coastal plains. South of the arid Sahara, there are vast savannas (grasslands). But the ancient surfaces of Africa are characterized by a wide variety of vegetation and by the disruption of spectacular geographical features such as the towering Drakensberg mountains in South Africa, and the Great Rift Valley in the East.

Most of Africa's mineral wealth is located in a series of tiny economic "islands": the petroleum fields of North and West Africa, the precious-metal reefs of Johannesburg and the Orange Free State, the copper-belt of Zambia and Zaire, the diamond deposits of Namibia and so on. Available minerals are mainly concentrated in southern Africa, which is the richest part not only of sub-Saharan Africa but of the continent as a whole.

However, a century ago, much of this treasure was jealously guarded by the earth. It was not until the discovery of gold and diamonds (Africa contributes 70-80 per cent of the world's production) that the continent began to attract foreign powers. These minerals, together with other raw materials, are vitally important for the industrialized countries' economies. Access to these resources was (and still is) one of the key reasons for the interest of external powers.

In such an enormous continent there are massive differences between its independent states: in terms of size, the Sudan's 2.5 million sq km (one million square miles) on the one hand, Burundi's 28,000 sq km (11,000 square miles) on the other; population – Nigeria with 90 million citizens, Guinea-Bissau and Swaziland with less than one million apiece; and annual income per head of population – $4,250 in Gabon, less than a fortieth of that in Chad. Population densities, political systems, educational facilities and life expectancies also illustrate the extreme contrasts between the 50 or so countries of modern Africa.

Theories of imperialism

What then were the causes of the partition (division) of Africa? Why was it that the Europeans suddenly decided to carve up the continent into huge African empires?

The answers to these questions are highly complex. One interpretation points to economic factors. Some European powers – notably Spain, Portugal and Britain – had first come to Africa in the 16th and 17th centuries in search of slaves for their new colonies in the Americas. This cruel trade in human lives soon became an integral part of a "triangle" of profit, with ships leaving Europe laden with goods for exchange in Africa for slaves, then traveling across the Atlantic, where the slaves would be sold and lucrative cargoes of sugar or tobacco taken on board for shipment back to Europe. Millions of Africans suffered before the trade was stopped in the early 19th century, but by then new pressures had arisen to ensure continued European interest in the continent. The Industrial Revolution and the dynamic growth of European industry required new markets and fresh sources of raw materials. Europeans wished to expand trade with Africa by importing raw materials in exchange for manufactured goods.

Another explanation emphasizes the growing importance of nationalism in Europe. People felt great pride in their country's achievements and thought this gave them the right to rule over "inferior" peoples. Germany and Italy had become united countries in 1870 and 1871 respectively. In order to assert their new identities, both attempted to grab African territories. To protect their own interests from this aggressive nationalism, Britain and France reacted in similar fashion. This empire-building or "imperialism" was extremely popular with the European peoples.

A third interpretation stresses strategic factors. The British invaded Egypt in 1882 with a view to protecting the route to the "Jewel in the Crown" of its empire – India. This sparked off a general "scramble" for African colonies. In 1869 the Suez Canal had been opened, and this became the shortest and most important route between Britain and India. Since Egypt was dependent on the waters of the Nile, Great Britain tried to prevent other powers from establishing colonies in the region. To achieve this, the British eventually took control of the Sudan, Kenya and Uganda.

A fourth theory sees partition as arising from the activities of "men on the spot." For religious, business and military reasons, explorers, soldiers, missionaries and adventurers convinced their mother countries to extend their rule in Africa.

A final interpretation is that which explains the partition in terms of African initiatives. Chiefs often made treaties and demanded protection in order to gain advantages in squabbles with traditional enemies. Sometimes they attempted to play off one European power against another. This local activity has been described as a "Scramble for protection."

In many cases, however, the seizure of African lands was the result of a variety of motives and ambitions. For instance, British interests in the Cape area (South Africa) were both strategic (to protect the route to India and beyond) and commercial. On the other hand, Italy's role in the "Scramble for Africa" seems to have been guided by an extreme nationalism, and dreams of recreating a modern Roman Empire. Similarly, France's humiliating defeat in the 1870-71 Franco-Prussian War helps to explain its search for prestige elsewhere.

The Scramble for Africa: British imperial forces annex Ado, northern Nigeria, 1891.

The European occupation

By 1900 Europe had divided up the greater part of the continent into formal colonial empires. So rapid had been the European advance that 80 per cent of Africa was subject to their authority. For the most part, this process had occurred through diplomatic agreements between the colonial powers. An international conference, summoned by the German Chancellor, Count Otto von Bismarck at Berlin in 1884-85, laid down the ground rules for the "effective occupation" of Africa. It provided the framework that permitted Europeans to divide the "Dark Continent" without major wars among themselves.

It was agreed that a European power could only claim African territory if it could demonstrate that it actually administered it. The conference did not partition the continent along precise boundaries as is commonly believed. Instead, it defined spheres of influence near the coast, leaving vast areas unallocated to any European state. Later treaties enabled exact boundaries to be marked out.

During the next 15 years, the European rivals moved rapidly into the interior as merchants, missionaries and military expeditions discovered worlds to conquer. By 1900 seven European powers – Britain, France, Belgium, Portugal, Germany, Italy and Spain – had established effective occupations over the whole continent.

This magnificent African cake

Although accomplished very swiftly, the division of Africa did not occur overnight. "Creeping partition" had been going on for some time. By the beginning of the 20th century, however, the scramble was virtually complete. With the exceptions of Ethiopia and Liberia (the latter of which was founded by freed slaves from the United States in the 1820s and recognized as an independent state in 1847), the continent was now under European control. What was called effective occupation had begun. Although Egypt was still nominally Turkish, it was under British protection. The Sudan was ruled jointly by Britain and Egypt.

The rest of Africa had been parceled out among the seven European colonial states. Of all the powers involved, France emerged with the lion's share of land by area. Spain had the least territory, most of which was desert or mosquito-infested tropical rain forest.

In many cases the division of "this magnificent African cake," as King Leopold II of the Belgians called it, was done with very little knowledge of what was being shared out.

Anti-colonial resistance

These lines on the map of Africa had been made good by force – as well as by developments in steam transport and anti-malarial drugs – and they had to be maintained by force. The military armaments and organization of the European powers were vastly superior to those of Africans. Spears, arrows and clubs were no match for rifles, artillery and machine guns.

As the colonial governments extended their rule they constantly encountered resistance. Sizable forces were used to deal with this. One of the most widespread revolts occurred in German East Africa. The Germans imposed their rule with such ruthlessness that it led to the bloody Maji Maji rebellion (1905-07). This was named after the fact that rebels swallowed medicine which was supposed to turn the bullets to water (*maji*).

In southern Africa there were two major struggles: between whites and blacks (especially between British forces and Cetewayo's Zulu warriors), and between the British and the Afrikaner Boers (descendants of the original Dutch settlers who first arrived at the Cape of Good Hope in 1652).

Cetewayo, a great Zulu warrior leader

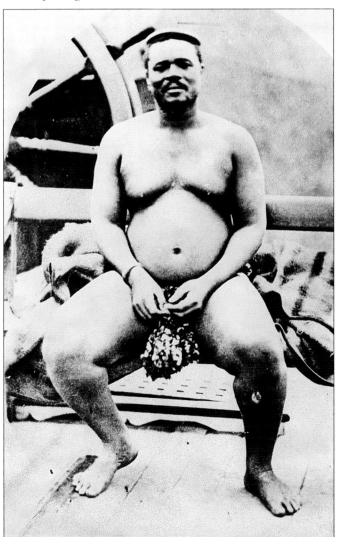

The growing conflict of interests between British imperialism and Afrikaner nationalism led to the Boer War of 1899-1902. The Boers were eventually defeated and their two republics were unified with Natal and the Cape Province in the 1910 Act of Union. South Africa remained part of the British Empire and subsequent Commonwealth for the next 50 years. While European armies (which were in fact predominantly black in composition) had numerous advantages over their larger African counterparts, it should not be forgotten that they also suffered a number of defeats. Two examples are the Zulu victory over the British at Isandhlwana (1879) and the Italian defeat at the hands of the Ethiopians at the Battle of Adowa (1896).

Internal revolts

Yet colonial conquest did not put an end to armed uprisings. There were numerous revolts in the period between 1900 and 1918. The prolonged resistance of the Baoule against French rule in the Ivory Coast (1901-17), the Zulu revolt in Natal (1906) and the Giriama-British War in Kenya (1914-15) are just three such instances. In certain parts of West Africa the colonial authorities were still fighting to subdue rebellions until the third decade of the century. For instance, military resistance in the French colony of Niger lasted until 1922.

However, conflict in the early part of the 20th century was not always bloody. The *Kyanyangire* ("refuse") revolt in western Uganda in 1907 was a classic example of unarmed resistance. Planned in strict secrecy, its leader Byabachwezi insisted on no violence. These actions resulted in concessions from the British imperial authorities.

The First World War

When Britain declared war on Germany in 1914, there were hopes that Africa would remain outside the conflict. But this was not to be. The colonial governments recruited more than one million Africans as soldiers, porters and laborers. While the African campaigns did not affect the course of the First World War (1914-18), they had a major impact on Africa itself. Except for Ethiopia and the Spanish territories, which remained neutral, the entire continent was sucked into the conflict. Black troops were used not only in Africa, but also in Europe and the Middle East. British and French colonial forces in West Africa quickly seized the small German colony of Togo in 1914, encountering little opposition.

Afrikaner guerrilla commandos make camp near Ladysmith during the 1899-1902 Boer War.

The task of overrunning the larger German colony of the Cameroons (by 1916) was much more difficult. In both cases, the purpose was to deny the Germans the use of their ports. Both territories were divided between Britain and France.

South African and Rhodesian forces conquered German Southwest Africa (in 1916), which effectively became a fifth province of the South African Union. For the remainder of the war, the unorthodox General Paul von Lettow-Vorbeck defended German East Africa against attacks from all sides. With only 5,000 German soldiers, he pinned down some 130,000 British, Belgian and South African troops in a masterful guerrilla campaign. He surrendered only when informed that Germany had signed an armistice.

Repartition

The principal political consequence of these hostilities was a partial repartition of Africa in which Germany lost its African colonies. In theory the four ex-German territories were placed under the trusteeship of an international organization, the League of Nations. In fact the spoils were parceled out among the victorious Allied powers. As a result Britain found herself the owner of a larger empire than at any time in her history.

The First World War caused much suffering to the African peoples, vast numbers of whom were involved, directly or indirectly, economically or militarily, in the conflict. The war also triggered off widespread revolts in Nigeria and French West Africa. This meant that substantial numbers of British and French troops, who would have otherwise been fighting on the Western Front in Europe, were engaged in "pacification" duties. For the most part, these uprisings were the final splutters of violent opposition to colonial rule until after the Second World War.

The interwar years

In the interwar era, protest against the colonial authorities was almost entirely peaceful. Frequently referred to as "secondary resistance," its supporters tried to obtain a greater say in running their colony through changes in the constitution and new laws. The organizations behind this movement were trade and educational associations, church groups, labor unions, debating societies and welfare organizations. Their methods were in stark contrast to armed "primary resistance" (before 1918).

During this "high noon" of the colonial period, the imperial powers consolidated their authority and mili-

tary administrators gave way to civilian governors. However, there were some major differences between how European powers ran their colonies. The main distinction was between the British, who pursued a policy of "indirect rule," and the other colonial powers – especially the French – who favored "direct rule."

Indirect rule

Britain economized by making as much use as possible of African chiefs. The policy owed much to Lord Lugard's ideas and experiences in northern Nigeria. Since there were so few men on the ground, administrators such as Lugard exercised power indirectly through traditional leaders.

Thus Africans were encouraged to develop their own institutions. Under this system of "indirect rule," the British claimed to interfere with the "native authorities" as little as possible. In reality, however, the chiefs' authority was undermined since British "advisers" were attached to their courts.

Direct rule

By contrast, the French constitution declared that "all men, without distinction of color, domiciled in French colonies, are French citizens and enjoy all the rights." Theoretically, citizenship was open to any individual who assimilated himself by education, speech and custom to the French lifestyle. Yet, as a number of writers have noted, had the French granted citizenship to all their colonial peoples, African representation in the Paris National Assembly would have outnumbered the French – a situation which could not be permitted.

At the same time, France believed in "direct rule." They employed many more administrative officers than did the British. Local government was run on orders from the central government and African chiefs were either ignored or bypassed.

Blacks and whites

In fact each country's colonial system adapted to local political circumstances in the territory involved. Yet however much "direct" and "indirect" rule differed, the colonial era did little or nothing to close the technological and economic gap between whites and blacks. On the contrary, the divide between the invaders and the invaded steadily widened. Meanwhile, Africans had lost their independence to an alien European culture. Social discrimination and color-bars (separation of blacks and whites) heightened the sense of racial injustice.

In every African possession a colonial economy was developed in which the modern sector was organized around the production of a few raw materials: groundnuts in the Gambia, copper in the Congo, palm products in Dahomey and so on. For the most part, such production was shaped to the requirements of Europe rather than to the needs of Africa itself.

The continent's mineral wealth was developed by international concerns, and commerce came to be dominated by a handful of foreign enterprises. Although the European powers acknowledged that they should help in the development of the continent, African nationalists complained that their lands were being exploited to serve outside interests.

Today it is commonplace to criticize the evils of colonialism, but there were some positive aspects. Colonialism brought political stability to the continent and gave it many economic benefits. An end was put to the slave trade (which was progressively replaced in the early years of the 19th century by the market in raw materials) and certain barbaric practices – such as the killing of twin babies and human sacrifices – were stamped out. Standards of living soared and there were great advances in medicine, hygiene and education.

Rightly or wrongly, many colonialists – missionaries, doctors, administrators and employers – saw themselves as the paternalistic bearers of Christian virtues and civilized standards. To the men and women of the early 1900s, their actions were justified by the superiority of Western civilization and the perceived backwardness of the "Dark Continent."

Even so, the imposition of foreign rule inevitably alienated the local people, destroying traditional ways of life and introducing alien cultural, economic, religious and political beliefs, often with the use or threat of force. Sparked in many cases by Western-style education and fueled by the widening experience of Africans in world affairs, the concept of nationalism emerged, building up pressures which few of the colonial powers could sustain.

German settlers befriend villagers in Southwest Africa (now known as Namibia), 1938.

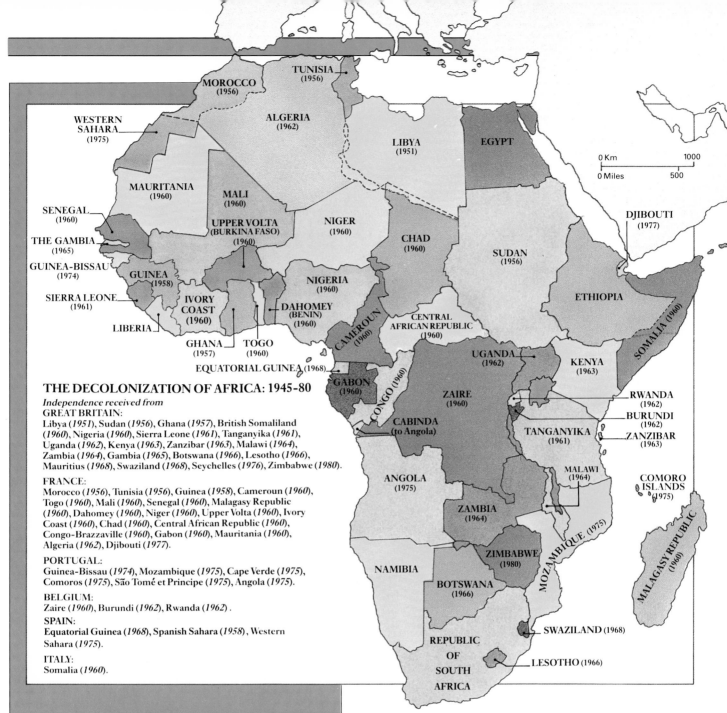

THE DECOLONIZATION OF AFRICA: 1945-80

Independence received from

GREAT BRITAIN:
Libya (*1951*), Sudan (*1956*), Ghana (*1957*), British Somaliland (*1960*), Nigeria (*1960*), Sierra Leone (*1961*), Tanganyika (*1961*), Uganda (*1962*), Kenya (*1963*), Zanzibar (*1963*), Malawi (*1964*), Zambia (*1964*), Gambia (*1965*), Botswana (*1966*), Lesotho (*1966*), Mauritius (*1968*), Swaziland (*1968*), Seychelles (*1976*), Zimbabwe (*1980*).

FRANCE:
Morocco (*1956*), Tunisia (*1956*), Guinea (*1958*), Cameroun (*1960*), Togo (*1960*), Mali (*1960*), Senegal (*1960*), Malagasy Republic (*1960*), Dahomey (*1960*), Niger (*1960*), Upper Volta (*1960*), Ivory Coast (*1960*), Chad (*1960*), Central African Republic (*1960*), Congo-Brazzaville (*1960*), Gabon (*1960*), Mauritania (*1960*), Algeria (*1962*), Djibouti (*1977*).

PORTUGAL:
Guinea-Bissau (*1974*), Mozambique (*1975*), Cape Verde (*1975*), Comoros (*1975*), São Tomé et Principe (*1975*), Angola (*1975*).

BELGIUM:
Zaire (*1960*), Burundi (*1962*), Rwanda (*1962*).

SPAIN:
Equatorial Guinea (*1968*), Spanish Sahara (*1958*), Western Sahara (*1975*).

ITALY:
Somalia (*1960*).

CHAPTER 2
THE ROAD TO INDEPENDENCE

Once the pressures for decolonization emerged in Africa, the process of European departure was remarkably fast, creating some 50 "new" states in less than 30 years. The withdrawal began in North Africa in the 1950s, culminating in the departure of the Portuguese in 1975 and the creation of Zimbabwe five years later. But South Africa, with its policies of racial segregation, remained.

A combination of factors contributed to the pace of decolonization. These included economic and educational developments within Africa, the Second World War, the Atlantic Charter, the independence of India, and the emergence of two "anti-colonial" superpowers, the United States and the Soviet Union.

African nationalism

The imperial retreat can be explained partly by the rise of nationalism within the colonies. "Nationalism" is usually associated with a struggle of a people for self-determination or self-rule. What makes nationalism in Africa so different is the fact that there are hardly any real nation-states in Africa.

Nigeria and Uganda, for example, did not exist before the 20th century. Their borders are the arbitrary creations of European statesmen and colonial administrators. Despite this, nationalist pressure was one of the key factors in the process of decolonization.

A number of reasons explain the rapid spread of African nationalism. One of these was education, which had produced a new generation of literate and educated Africans. Many of the most able were educated in Europe itself. Future African leaders like Kwame Nkrumah, Jomo Kenyatta, Léopold Senghor and Félix Houphouët-Boigny were accustomed to the life and talk of London or Paris, where the principles of freedom and political independence were openly discussed. As this took place in the capitals of the major colonial powers, the views rarely reflected those of established authority: frequently, they centered around the anti-capitalist philosophy of Karl Marx. These views became known as communism and were based on the idea of the collective ownership of industry and agriculture. Although few African nationalists became confirmed communists, their views reflected an anti-European slant.

Newspapers also made their appearance in Africa on

Kwame Nkrumah, Ghana's first leader, 1953.

a considerable scale. Carrying news of the wider world, they too had their impact. Economic developments had also led to the growth of an African working class. The students and the working class were highly receptive to new political ideas and outside influences. Ironically, because the imperial powers needed local educated and skilled manpower, they helped to sow the very seeds of their own removal. Education was thus a moving force behind the desire for self-rule.

The nationalist movements were also encouraged by the fate of peoples elsewhere in the world. If India, which received its independence from Britain in 1947, could be free, why not Africa? Thus nationalist victories in Asia provided inspiration and guidelines for the African nationalists. A further argument was the fact that Ethiopia and Liberia ruled themselves.

The issue of race also played a role in the rise of nationalist feeling. Many Africans felt humiliated by the foreign occupation of their land and the ideas of white racial superiority. They began to demand the same privileges as whites, some of whom treated blacks as inferior beings. The search for racial equality was part and parcel of the nationalist upsurge.

THE SECOND WORLD WAR

Probably the greatest catalyst of all was the impact of the Second World War (1939-45). It marked a turning point in the colonial history of Africa, and had a much greater effect on Africa than had the First World War.

The Second World War provided a powerful impetus for African political nationalism. This happened in a number of ways. First, in Article 3 of the Atlantic Charter, the Allies promised to respect "the right of all peoples to choose the form of government under which they live." Although some European politicians claimed this only applied to Nazi-occupied Europe, the United States and the British Labor Party insisted that it applied worldwide. The Soviet Union was equally hostile to colonialism and backed the United States in this matter.

Second, large numbers of Africans saw military service in the war, not only in Africa but more importantly overseas. From British territories alone, 375,000 Africans served in the British Army, often with distinction. The experience widened their political horizons and thousands returned home unwilling to accept previous conditions. Having fought alongside

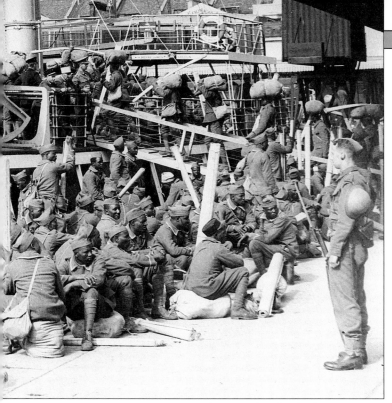

French colonial troops embark in England, 1940.

white men, many were convinced that they had earned the right to share in the government of their own countries. Ex-soldiers played a leading role in the subsequent struggle for independence.

Third, the fact that the two principal colonial powers in Africa, Britain and France, had been seriously weakened by the war, made the struggle that much easier. After 1945 they were to find it increasingly difficult to assemble the financial and military resources necessary to maintain their empires. In short, war had exhausted the European imperial states. For a variety of economic, social and political reasons, Africa's political masters gradually gave in to nationalist demands.

However, when the war ended in 1945 few could have foreseen the imminence of independence. Whereas prior to 1939 nationalists worked for change within the system, after 1945 they challenged the right of Britain, France and the others to govern them at all. The "Winds of Change," in the words of the British prime minister, Harold Macmillan, swept across the continent.

THE END OF BRITISH RULE

Opposition to imperial rule, which raged through postwar Africa, had its origins in Europe. In London, African leaders formulated plans for bringing independence to their people. Within the continent, nationalist fervor was growing.

Although Clement Attlee's Labor Government (1945-51) was in favor of transferring political power to its West African colonies, there was considerable conflict between Britain and the nationalists. There were two reasons for this. One was that there was disagreement on the pace of decolonization. The nationalists were impatient with the British view that it would take considerable time to train Africans in the business of running a country.

Second, the British authorities had been cultivating traditional chiefs for a major role in central government. But the chiefs were regarded by the new educated elite as too conservative. Nevertheless, despite these clashes, the British left most of their African territories on peaceful terms. Apart from the self-governing colony of Rhodesia (which will be discussed later), the only territory to experience major conflict before independence was Kenya.

Ghana's example

The first breakthrough came in West Africa in the colony known as the Gold Coast, which became Ghana. Ghana's Dr Kwame Nkrumah, who had been invited back from self-imposed exile to head the major nationalist party, demanded "Self-Government Now." His Convention People's Party (CPP) organized marches, demonstrations and boycotts. In 1948 an ex-soldiers' demonstration led to riots in the capital, Accra. This was followed by looting, shooting and deaths. The protests spread and more killings and injuries resulted. These upheavals were a great shock to the British colonial authorities, who believed the people there to be the happiest in Africa. If violence could happen there it could happen anywhere.

As a result of these events, Nkrumah was branded an "agitator" and imprisoned. After an enquiry he was released, but following further disturbances he was returned to James Fort prison in Accra. Far from hindering his campaign, Nkrumah's arrest turned him into a martyr.

It was from jail that the CPP won an overwhelming victory in Ghana's first national elections. The Governor, Sir Charles Arden-Clarke, had no alternative but to ask Nkrumah to head the first African administration in 1951. In March 1957, Ghana became independent as a full and equal member of the British Commonwealth, the organization linking Britain with her former colonies. That part of Togo which had been administered by Britain since the end of the First World War, voted in 1956 for union with Ghana.

Nigeria and Sierra Leone

This pattern of progress, with minor variations, was mirrored throughout British West Africa. After a delay which was resolved by the adoption of a federal constitution, Nigeria achieved independence under Nnamdi Azikiwe in October 1960.

In Sierra Leone, advancement toward black government was hindered by animosities between privileged Creoles (the descendants of freed slaves) around Freetown and the African tribes of the interior. Sir Milton Margai, who represented the "up-country" people of the hinterland, led his coastal state to independence in April 1961.

North Africa

Elsewhere on the continent, the African advance continued. The independence of (the former Anglo-Egyptian) Sudan came in 1956. Offered the option of union with Egypt or complete independence, the Muslim-dominated country became an independent republic on January 1.

Egypt's independence had been recognized by a treaty with Britain in 1936. However, the Egyptians did not regard themselves as being fully free until their nationalization of the Suez Canal Company and the failure of the Anglo-French landing at Port Said in 1956 during the Suez Crisis.

The three colonial territories seized from Italy during the Second World War, Eritrea, Libya and Italian Somaliland, had at first been placed under British administration. In 1952 one of these, Eritrea, was granted to Ethiopia by the United Nations as an "autonomous territory," retaining a degree of self-government. Libya, liberated by the Allies in 1943 and then ruled by the British and French, gained independence under King Idris in 1951.

Somalia was an unusual case. This was because it was a union of two colonies: British Somaliland and Italian Somaliland were combined and gained independence as a single state in 1960.

The creation of Tanzania

After 1945, powerful nationalist movements emerged throughout east and central Africa. Four times the size of Great Britain, Tanganyika was granted independence in December 1961. A decade earlier, the British had put forward the principle that power should be shared equally among all three races: blacks (8 million), Asians (70,000) and whites (20,000). This plan was totally opposed by the Tanganyika African National Union (TANU), founded in 1954. Its leader was the son of a chief, an Edinburgh University graduate and schoolteacher, Julius Nyerere.

After elections in 1958-59 and some unrest, the Governor, Sir Richard Turnbull, accepted that there should be an African government. Progress toward independence was accelerated. A crushing TANU victory at the 1960 elections ensured that Nyerere became prime minister in 1961.

Zanzibar, a British island possession off the coast of Tanganyika, became independent in December 1963. Only one month later, the Sultan of Zanzibar was deposed in a bloody revolution. The Sultan's Arab-dominated government was very unpopular with the African masses. Following a police mutiny, Sheikh Abedi Karume's Revolutionary Council came to power. Hundreds of people died in the subsequent rioting. Three months later, the two territories of Tanganyika and Zanzibar were unified to become the Republic of Tanzania, with Nyerere as its first president.

Uganda

In Uganda, where there were very few European settlers, there was little need for an anti-colonial struggle, since the British made it clear in 1950 that independence was on the agenda. In fact some parts of Uganda, for example the Kingdom of Buganda, had achieved self-government by 1945. However a new class of educated townsmen emerged which resented the power of the Kabaka (King) of Buganda. This led to much unrest, but when the colonial government tried to depose the Kabaka, all rival groups rallied to support him. Eventually Buganda and three other tribal monarchies were preserved in the constitution by the British when Uganda became independent in October 1962. Dr Milton Obote became prime minister and the Kabaka was appointed president.

Kenya

Unlike the relatively peaceful path to freedom taken by Uganda and Tanzania, the road to independence in Kenya was fraught with inter-racial strife. In contrast to West Africa, known as "the white man's grave," Kenya's idyllic climate had led to a considerable influx of white settlers. At the forefront of the nationalist struggle was Jomo Kenyatta, a well-educated man of imposing stature and personality. He was from one of Kenya's largest groups, the Kikuyu. In 1946 he was hailed as the leader of the Kenya African Union, a party which campaigned for "one man, one vote."

Under this system the Africans would have had an overwhelming majority in any election. The British administration's response in 1951 was to nominate six Africans to the Legislative Council, which was made up of 54 members.

The Mau Mau revolt

At this stage more and more Kikuyu began to turn to violence. Their primary grievance concerned the shortage of fertile land available to them, since much of it was reserved for white settlers. Many joined a secret organization with the mysterious name of "Mau Mau." Its objective was to drive out Europeans. At secret meetings deep in the forest, members swore elaborate oaths to kill whites and any blacks who collaborated with them.

Mau Mau groups developed tactics of guerrilla warfare. Armed mainly with *simis* (flat, double-edged swords) and axes, the basic tactic was the use of terror at night. Ghastly mutilations were the hallmark of Mau Mau operations.

In October 1952, Mau Mau's gruesome activity became sufficiently threatening for the government to announce a State of Emergency which lasted nearly eight years. Kenyatta and dozens of other African nationalists were arrested. They were charged, on patchy evidence, with "managing" the violence. For the first time in peace, British troops were flown into Kenya and strenuous efforts were made to arrest the Mau Mau leaders and destroy the movement. This proved to be a difficult task.

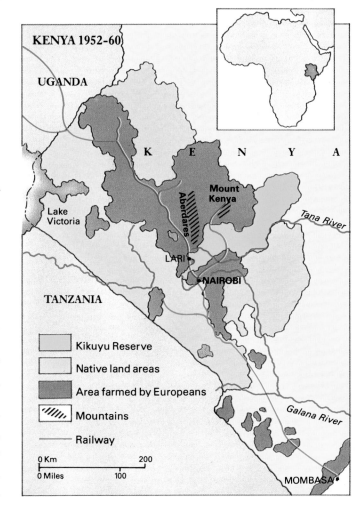

KENYA 1952-60

UGANDA

K E N Y A

Mount Kenya

Lake Victoria

Aberdares

Tana River

LARI

NAIROBI

TANZANIA

Galana River

MOMBASA

- Kikuyu Reserve
- Native land areas
- Area farmed by Europeans
- Mountains
- Railway

0 Km   200
0 Miles   100

Jomo Kenyatta is led into a Kenya courthouse in 1952 during the State of Emergency.

Mau Mau war camps in the densely wooded forest slopes of Mount Kenya and the Aberdares were supplied with food from rebel villages. Weapons were stolen from the security forces or produced by hidden arms workshops in the capital, Nairobi. Raids on European farms were followed by major attacks, to which the colonial government responded with great force. It was not simply a conflict between black and white, since neighboring groups frequently took the opportunity to settle old scores.

Counterinsurgency

The colonial regime employed a variety of techniques to defeat their opponents, known as counter-insurgency. These included the use of armored vehicles and artillery and the bombing of guerrilla camps in the hills. Mau Mau units were pursued by special tracker teams, and "pseudo-gangs" of captured or surrendered fighters were "turned" and sent back into the forests. They had to pose as Mau Mau gangs in order to contact and eliminate the enemy. Medicine men were also recruited to administer counteroaths.

In addition, protected villages were established in which scattered communities were uprooted and moved to centrally located settlements in order to deny food, supplies and shelter to the insurgents. At the height of the Emergency, when 13,000 rebels were engaged in anti-government activities, the colonial forces employed 11 infantry battalions, 21,000 police and a Kikuyu Home Guard some 25,000 strong.

The effectiveness of these counterinsurgency methods was enhanced by divisions within the Kikuyu people. Some of them saw the Mau Mau forces as "freedom fighters," but others believed that terror tactics would destroy any chance of political progress. Thousands of Kikuyu were murdered because they assisted the government. Of all these killings, the most notorious was the Lari massacre which took place in March 1953. On that occasion the inhabitants of several villages were hacked and burned to death by a large gang of armed insurgents.

The security services took more than three years to break up and isolate the rebels in the hills. It was not until October 1956 that the main counteroffensive came to a halt. According to the official figures, the government forces killed 7,800 rebels and lost over 500 of their own men, most of whom were Africans. Another 2,000 Kenyans were killed by Mau Mau.

A shantytown in Nairobi, Kenya, 1952. Such areas were fertile territory for the recruitment of Mau Mau guerrillas.

Order was re-established in the tribal areas and the authorities embarked on a vigorous policy of land reform, guaranteeing ownership to native Kenyans in rural areas. At the same time the British government decided to hasten the pace of political reform. Nevertheless, sporadic guerrilla warfare continued for another four years until 1960, when the State of Emergency ended.

Despite opposition from European settlers, independence was now the main issue in Kenyan politics. A 1960 conference provided for an elected African majority in the Legislative Council. Finally, in 1961, Kenyatta was released from detention to become Kenya's first prime minister at independence in December 1963.

Central African Federation

Farther south, the British government combined the two Rhodesias and Nyasaland in 1953 to form the Central African Federation. European settlers there believed that the whole unit would benefit economically. They also hoped it would make it easier to maintain white rule. The European view was that franchise (voting) restrictions were necessary to ensure that only "civilized and responsible persons" could vote.

From the start, Africans vigorously opposed the Federation. They saw it, correctly, as a means of maintaining white supremacy. In Northern Rhodesia (Zambia), Kenneth Kaunda, the son of a missionary, founded the Zambia African National Congress. In the same year, 1958, Dr Hastings Banda of Nyasaland (Malawi) took over the leadership of the Nyasaland African Congress. Both Congresses were militant and their leaders decided that working within the existing political system would achieve little or nothing.

Instead, they used such methods as demonstrations, strikes, and passive resistance. In turn, these were met with government action: states of emergency, arrests and detentions. Like Nkrumah of Ghana and Kenyatta of Kenya, Kaunda and Banda became "prison graduates" during the last phase of colonial rule.

In view of African opposition to the Federation, Britain appointed a Royal Commission under Lord Monckton to investigate. It recommended drastic changes. These led to African majorities on the Legislative Councils in Nyasaland and Northern Rhodesia and independence as Malawi and Zambia, respectively under Banda and Kaunda, in July and October 1964. This left Southern Rhodesia – now called simply Rhodesia – on its own.

THE END OF FRENCH RULE

The French had actively discouraged nationalist politics. They had taken immense trouble to teach the French language and culture to their colonial peoples. Unlike the British, the French did not at first accept the idea of independent African states. After the Second World War, wide-ranging reforms were introduced and in 1946 most French possessions in Africa were given the status of "overseas territories" of France. African leaders from each colony were elected to the National Assembly (parliament) in Paris.

For the most part, France's withdrawal from Africa was comparatively orderly. But decolonization encountered difficulties in Madagascar and in North Africa. Although most of the French colonies became independent in the space of just one year (14 in 1960), they might have had to wait much longer had it not been for French difficulties in Algeria.

West Africa

Postwar political developments in British West Africa influenced events in neighboring French territory. In order to stave off demands for independence, the French government passed the *loi cadre* ("outline law") in 1956. It was an enabling act permitting its overseas territories a considerable degree of local self-rule. Elected assemblies were set up in each of France's colonies. This meant that the huge West African Federation was divided up into eight units: Senegal, Guinea, Ivory Coast, Togo, Dahomey (later Benin), Mali, Upper Volta (later Burkina Faso) and Niger. Previously, France's West African territories had been administered from Dakar.

This new policy was strongly supported by Houphouët-Boigny of the Ivory Coast. He served in the French Cabinet (the group of ministers in a government) in Paris from 1956 to 1959. It was vigorously denounced by Senghor of Senegal, who had visions of a large West African federal republic.

When General de Gaulle returned to power in May 1958 he offered the French colonies a choice. They could either pull away from French rule and sever all links with Paris or they could join France in the formation of a new *Union Française* ("French Community"). Under this system, France would control economic, defense and foreign policy, while the member states would have internal self-government.

The terms for the first option were forbidding. Any colony that opted for immediate independence would have all political, economic and educational ties cut.

In the event only Sékou Touré's Guinea voted for total independence. "We prefer poverty in freedom to riches in slavery," was Touré's explanation.

Yet he did not anticipate that the French reaction would be quite so severe. De Gaulle decided that Guinean independence should be interpreted literally: all French administrators, teachers and technicians were immediately pulled out. They took most of their equipment with them. Within days French financial aid came to an end.

All the other West African colonies chose membership of the *Union Française*. In 1960, however, they were rewarded when France granted full independence to the seven colonies. Some of them had become discontented and the French government decided it would be better to grant total independence before it was demanded by force.

French Equatorial Africa and Cameroun

The four territories of French Equatorial Africa (the Central African Republic, Chad, Congo and Gabon) also gained full independence in 1960. However, the road to independence for Cameroun (formerly the Cameroons) was different, complicated and violent. Administered by Britain and France under United Nations' trusteeship, ex-German Cameroun was divided in 1960-61. The French part became the independent Republic of Cameroun, under Ahmadu Ahidjo, a former telephone operator.

Before this was achieved, there was a large-scale rebellion by nationalist guerrillas. Led by Dr Félix Moumié, who followed the ideas of Karl Marx, they were fighting for the reunification of Cameroun. Much of the country was outside the government's control. For some time, the disorders were almost as serious a threat as the Mau Mau revolt had been to the British authorities in Kenya. It lasted for three years and was eventually subdued with the help of French troops. Over 10,000 civilians and at least 1,000 soldiers are said to have died during the bloodiest fighting for independence in French West Africa.

The two British parts of Cameroun, the Northern and Southern states, were offered a choice of joining either Nigeria or the Cameroun Republic. In 1961 Northern Cameroun voted to join Nigeria; Southern Cameroun elected to join the former French Cameroun in a federation.

Madagascar and the Horn

The armed rising of the Malagasy people against the French in March 1947 was organized by nationalist secret societies. It was provoked by the post-1945 restoration of French rule – Madagascar had been occupied by Britain during the Second World War to prevent its seizure by the Japanese. Another grievance of the Malagasy people was the economic exploitation of the island by the French.

The French authorities tried to counter the influence of the main nationalist organization by encouraging an alternative and more modern political party. The trigger for the uprising is obscure. Poorly equipped peasants and some ex-soldiers used spears, knives and stones. Encouraged by witchdoctors, armed rebels attacked French planters and administrators. Some 16,000 "collaborators" who worked with the colonial regime were also murdered. It took a year and a half of fighting to put down the revolt.

This was done with extreme severity and the rebellion's 20 military leaders were executed. No one is certain about the numbers killed. The French admitted to killing 11,000, but the nationalists claimed the figure was nearer 80,000. In addition, much of the island was devastated. After this, the progress to independence went remarkably smoothly. Internal autonomy was granted in 1957 and the Republic of Malagasy came into being in June 1960.

On the Horn of Africa, tiny French Somaliland was renamed the Territory of the Afars and the Issas (after the names of the two major groups) in 1968. Then in 1977, France's last colonial possession on the mainland of Africa became independent, changing its name to Djibouti.

Northwest Africa

In all three territories of Northwest Africa, nationalist aspirations were encouraged by developments in the Second World War. The German invasion of France in 1940 had demonstrated the weakness of a major colonial power and France suffered an enormous loss of prestige from her defeat. Most of the *Maghreb* (the Arabic word for "west") had fallen to the French: Algeria in 1830, Tunisia in 1881 and Morocco in 1912.

Morocco and Tunisia had a different status from Algeria. The former were protectorates, not an integral part of France. This meant that, unlike Algeria which had been part of France since 1848, they had no representation in Paris. But both territories were left with local, traditional rulers.

Nationalist movements in Morocco

With the exception of South Africa, no other part of the continent witnessed such a rapid build-up of white settlers as occurred in French North Africa. However, in none of these territories did the Arab Muslims willingly accept the forceful imposition of French rule. There had always been antagonism between the conquerors and the conquered. In all three countries, the nationalist struggle also had a religious character. Europeans were viewed as infidels (unbelievers), people inferior to the true believers of Islam.

Nationalist protest in Morocco began in 1930 when Mohammed Allal el-Fassi led violent demonstrations against French rule. By 1943 various nationalist groupings had merged to form the *Istiqlal* (Independence) Party, a traditionalist movement supported by Sultan Mohammed V. When he refused to condemn *Istiqlal*, he was deposed and exiled in 1953.

But the mass of the people continued to view him as their legitimate ruler and armed opposition grew in both town and countryside. France decided it could not deal with rebellion in both Algeria and Morocco. In March 1956 therefore, Morocco was granted independence. Spain followed suit and granted independence to her Moroccan territory but retained control of the two enclaves of Ceuta and Melilla. Morocco was now reunited under the Sultan, who was brought back to rule as King.

Tunisia's president, Habib Bourguiba.

Tunisia gains independence

In Tunisia during this period there was similar opposition to colonial rule. Led by a French-trained lawyer, Habib Bourguiba, the nationalists organized demonstrations. By 1954 they had begun to use violence. Although Bourguiba was a moderate, the French authorities regarded him as dangerous. He, too, spent long periods in prison or in exile.

As it became more and more difficult to govern through a puppet ruler, the Dey, France decided to grant internal autonomy (in 1954) and then independence (in 1956). The traditional monarchy was abolished and Bourguiba became president.

Algeria

Whereas Morocco and Tunisia had originally been occupied through diplomacy rather than force, the conquest of Algeria in the 19th century took nearly three decades. The process had been as cruel as it had been prolonged. By 1945 Algeria had the largest European population in Africa, after South Africa.

Even before the Second World War the French settlers (*colons*) opposed demands for equality and the removal of discrimination. This fueled anti-French feeling and led to increasing demands by Algerian nationalists.

However, there had been anti-French rioting in the town of Sétif in May 1945. On VE day (celebrating Victory in Europe against the Germans), Muslim nationalists carried banners alongside Allied flags. The placards read "Down with Colonialism" and "Long Live a Free Algeria." Police seized the banners, scuffles broke out and a full-scale battle began. The savage attacks left 88 dead and wounded. The French retaliated with great brutality and at least 1,900 Algerians were killed.

For some years after these events the French believed that their strong policy had driven the more extreme nationalists into exile. However, Algeria was to endure a bitter war of independence lasting over seven years. It contained all the elements of horror experienced in Kenya.

ALGERIA 1960

ALGIERS
PHILIPPEVILLE
ORAN
TUNIS
SETIF
BISKRA
Morice Line
TUNISIA
TOUGGOURT
A L G E R I A
LIBYA
IN SALAH

Areas of FLN activity
▲ Oil-producing areas
• • • Natural gas pipeline
– – – Oil pipelines
– – – French defensive lines

0 Km   800
0 Miles   500

By the early 1950s, the maintenance of the political *status quo* – in which the country was legally an integral part of France – was becoming increasingly unacceptable to the majority of Algerian Muslims. Secret preparations for a rebellion were being made by a revolutionary committee that became the nucleus of the *Front de Libération Nationale* (National Liberation Front – FLN). One of the leaders was a former French Army sergeant who had been decorated for bravery. His name was Ahmed Ben Bella. In time he was to become the first President of Algeria.

The Algerian War

The Algerian War of Independence broke out on November 1, 1954, when the FLN coordinated 70 armed

French troops control people moving in and out of Arab areas of Algiers during the FLN bombing campaign, 1957.

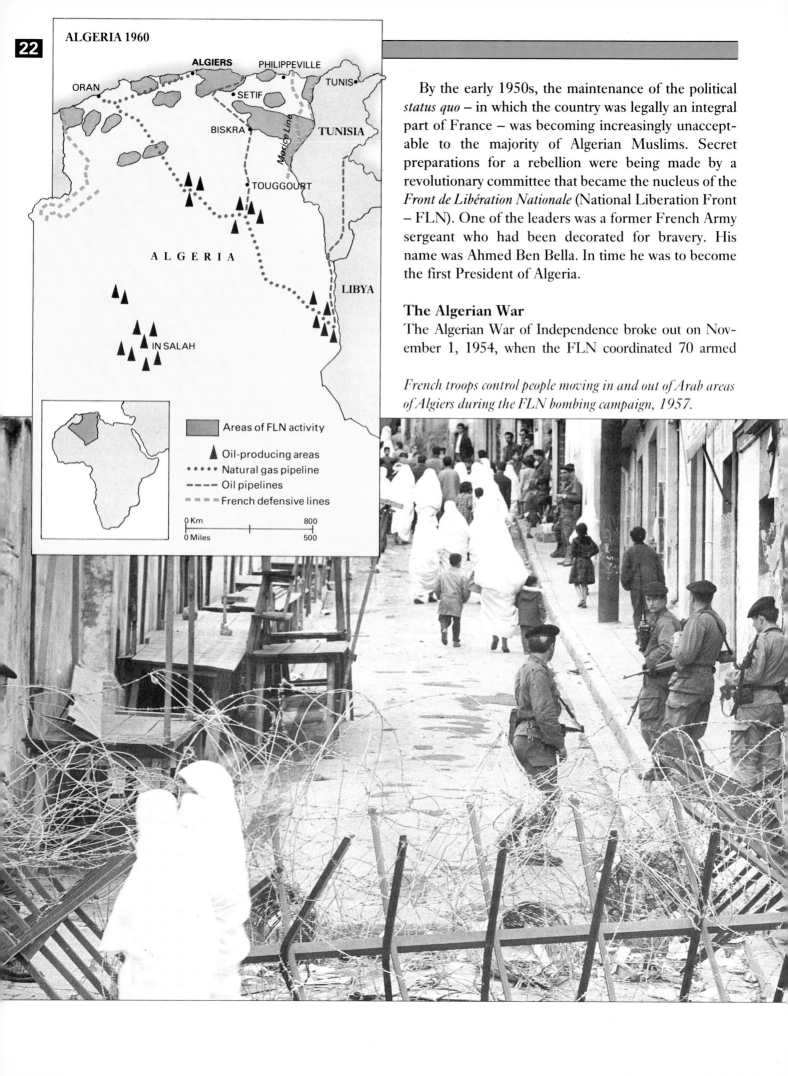

attacks on European homes, government buildings, police posts and railway tracks. To begin with, these military operations were sporadic and unsuccessful but by the summer of 1956 the guerrillas had built up a force of 20,000 fighters, many of whom were experienced ex-servicemen. They controlled large areas of inaccessible countryside and, because the majority of the population supported them, the supply of recruits to replace losses seemed inexhaustible. Six months later the FLN moved into the towns in strength and received considerable funding and weapons from Egypt, Morocco and other Arab states.

The ferocity of the conflict escalated when French paratroops under General Jacques Massu swept into Algiers in January 1957. In house-to-house searches and mass arrests, thousands of Algerians were picked up for brutal interrogation. Meanwhile squads of *colons* extracted their own bloody revenge against suspected terrorists. Their "tit-for-tat" retaliations accounted for some 12,000 deaths.

French counterinsurgency strategy also included efforts designed to win the "hearts and minds" of the population through development programs administered by Special Administrative Section (SAS) officers. However, the destruction of entire villages by French forces to punish FLN supporters, and widespread allegations of torture, merely hardened anti-French feeling.

De Gaulle comes to power

With 250,000 troops in Algeria by 1958, the French began to get the upper hand – at least militarily, but they could not eradicate the nationalist fervor for independence. On the other hand, after four years of war the *colons* were more determined than ever to keep Algeria French. Significant elements within the French Army, especially those like the paratroops (*les paras*) who had been at the forefront of the fighting, had come to share their views.

Fearful that the government in Paris was about to betray them, the *colons* staged a revolt in Algiers in May 1958, with the connivance of sympathetic army units. These events toppled the French government, bringing Charles de Gaulle to power as head of the Fifth Republic. He realized that a military solution was impossible, and moved Algeria toward independence, which was achieved in July 1962.

The nationalist victory had been achieved at an awesome cost: at least a million Algerians – 10 per cent of the population – lost their lives. Half a million widows and a quarter of a million orphans were left. By contrast, about 17,500 French troops and almost 3,000 *colons* died. Fought by a well-organized nationalist group, it was the bloodiest struggle in colonial Africa.

BELGIAN AFRICA

The transfer of rule from a colonial power to an independent African government occurred more suddenly in the Belgian Congo than in any other country. Compared with most other colonies, the Congo was already rich. It had copper mines, tin, uranium, silver, diamonds and rubber. With this wealth, the Belgians established an excellent health and welfare system for their African subjects. Social conditions were improved but black efforts to gain more political power were resisted. The few strikes and demonstrations that did occur were quickly crushed by the *Force Publique*, a strong and well-trained security force.

The Belgians believed that their enlightened policy would prevent the development of nationalist feelings. This was not the case. It was impossible to keep the Congolese ignorant of developments in Nkrumah's Ghana, which gained independence in 1957. In 1958 an independence movement, the Congolese National Movement, was founded which took the Belgians completely by surprise.

Although local government reform in the larger towns had been introduced in 1957, urban riots broke out in January 1959. During the next few months the colonial administration lost control of large areas of their vast possession.

The Belgian authorities were faced with two alternatives: repression or political concessions. They chose the latter course of action. Political parties sprang up and the colonial government negotiated a rapid move to independence. This took place in June 1960 with Patrice Lumumba as prime minister and Joseph Kasavubu as president.

Belgium's other colonial possessions – the tiny, impoverished highland territories of Burundi and Rwanda – were granted independence in July 1962. Having learned their lesson in the Congo, the Belgians took precautions to ensure that the transfer was peaceful. But this did not prevent the emergence of deep-seated ethnic animosities after 1962. In both states post-independence has been a grim story of assassination, massacre and genocide.

PORTUGAL'S COLONIAL WARS

By the late 1960s European rule was a thing of the past for most of the continent, but not in the southern part of Africa. Portugal, the first European colonizer in Africa, seemed determined to pursue a policy of "first in, last out."

Portugal was a right-wing country which could ill afford to lose its colonies. It was too weak economically to decolonize. After years of neglect, the main Portuguese possessions of Mozambique and Angola were proving to be valuable assets. Oil fields had been discovered in Angola.

In order to strengthen its grip on the territories, Portugal's government promoted large-scale white settlement. By 1970 Mozambique and Angola had a combined white population of half a million. However, this European influx did not prevent anti-colonial wars that began in Angola (1961) and Mozambique (1964), as well as in Portugal's West African colony of Guinea-Bissau (1963).

Angola

Although major uprisings in Angola had been ruthlessly suppressed in the 1920s as well as in 1935, the nationalist flame had not been extinguished. Against a background of widespread black unemployment and blatant discrimination against blacks, several rebellions broke out in Angola.

The first took place in the cotton fields; the second occurred in the capital, Luanda, where police stations and government buildings were attacked. A large rural settler influx led to a further uprising in the coffee-growing northeast of the country. This spontaneous peasant revolt escalated into terrible violence. Hundreds of European and *mesticos* (mixed race) were massacred. The government's reaction was swift. Barbarities were met with barbarities.

For the next 13 years the violence continued. It was much longer than, and at times certainly as brutal as, the war in Algeria. However, the fighting was complicated by the existence of three liberation movements. Each of these was supported by one of three major tribal groups in Angola.

Angolan children sit on a Portuguese colonialist's statue, toppled by UNITA rebels in the War of Independence.

The National Front for the Liberation of Angola (FNLA) was led by Holden Roberto. Dr Agostinho Neto's Popular Movement for the Liberation of Angola (MPLA) was the second group, drawing its support from Luanda. In June 1960, the MPLA had petitioned the Portuguese to introduce political reforms; their response was to arrest MPLA leaders and to have Neto publicly flogged. After that, the MPLA turned for support to the Soviet Union, sending guerrilla recruits to eastern Europe and Cuba for training and receiving arms from the communist bloc. The third movement was Jonas Savimbi's Union for the Total Independence of Angola (UNITA), formed in southern Angola from rebels within the FNLA and eventually supported by South Africa.

Mozambique and Guinea-Bissau

Organized resistance to Portuguese authority in Mozambique flared up in 1964 when the Mozambique Liberation Front (known as FRELIMO) embarked on an armed revolutionary campaign. To begin with, FRELIMO was led by Eduardo Mondlane. He met his death in 1969 when he was blown up by a parcel bomb allegedly sent by Portuguese agents. He was replaced as leader by Samora Machel, Mozambique's first African president.

In Guinea-Bissau the armed struggle against Portuguese colonial rule was led by the African Independence Party of Guinea and Cape Verde (PAIGC). The party was established by Amilcar Cabral, an agricultural engineer. From 1963 he initiated widespread guerrilla attacks on the Portuguese. In January 1974, Cabral was assassinated by PAIGC dissidents widely believed to be in the pay of the Portuguese.

Considerable Portuguese resources were deployed in their wars against the guerrillas. In terms of manpower, they involved a massive burden of 140,000 troops: 50,000 each in Mozambique and Angola, and 40,000 in Guinea. In addition, large numbers of Africans were employed by the security forces. Many of these were recruited into specialist counterinsurgency units where they gained a fearsome reputation. The Portuguese secret police (PIDE) was also highly effective in eliminating political enemies.

The end of Portuguese rule

While the nationalist forces had achieved a good deal by 1974, they were not able to force a conclusion. Then the wars suddenly ended when Portuguese officers in Lisbon overthrew the dictator, Marcello Caetano.

Determined to end colonial conflicts that had already killed 8,000 Portuguese troops and were gobbling up almost half of Lisbon's annual budget, radical officers installed General Antonio de Spinola in power. A former governor of Guinea-Bissau, he had been dismissed by Caetano for publishing a book, *Portugal and the Future*. In this he had advocated a political rather than a military solution in Africa. The Lisbon coup caused the entire colonial administration to fall into disarray and the transfer of power was quickly negotiated.

Guinea's independence was recognized in September 1974, Mozambique's in June 1975. Independence came to Angola in November 1975 when a transitional government made up of the three rival factions was formed. The stage was set for the Angolan civil war. After an uninterrupted presence in Africa of 500 years, Portugal's departure resulted not so much from defeat on the continent itself but from political developments in the mother country.

The last European power to leave its mainland African empire was Spain. It granted independence to Equatorial Guinea in October 1968, and started to evacuate its Spanish Sahara possession in 1975 (it was promptly annexed by Morocco and Mauritania). This left the two tiny territories of Ceuta and Melilla in Spain's possession, an issue still to be resolved with Morocco.

Mozambique's Samora Machel.

THE SOUTHERN REDOUBTS

The three territories of Bechuanaland, Basutoland and Swaziland had become British protectorates in the 19th century. Their transfer to South Africa, which had been envisaged in 1909, was again proposed by the South African government after the Second World War. But the emergence of apartheid (separate racial development) in South Africa ensured Britain's refusal to entertain any such union. As a result, and with very little black nationalist prompting, the three countries attained independent statehood as Botswana (under Sir Seretse Khama) in 1966, Lesotho (under Chief Leabua Jonathan) in 1966 and Swaziland (under King Sobhuza II) in 1968.

To the north of South Africa lay Rhodesia. Nominally a British colony, it was in practice administered by a small white minority. The colonists (in the true sense of the word, that is, permanent settlers) were determined to prevent "their" country going the way of Zambia, Kenya and the others.

Rhodesia's UDI

Although Britain had granted internal self-government to Rhodesia's European settlers in 1923, she was still the nominal colonial power. Britain remained legally responsible for the colony's foreign affairs and had the right (never exercised) to veto any laws passed by the settlers. The white Rhodesians were bitterly disappointed by London's refusal to grant them total independence. Instead the British government outlined proposals for black majority rule in the distant future. Long drawn-out negotiations came to nothing.

Recognizing the threat, the whites sought to entrench their position with a Unilateral Declaration of Independence (UDI) in November 1965. Under the leadership of Ian Smith, the Rhodesians cut off links with Britain. Harold Wilson's Labor Government was not willing to use military force to overthrow Smith's illegal regime. Attempts to settle the dispute by Mr Smith and Prime Minister Wilson on board the British warships HMS *Tiger* and HMS *Fearless*, in 1966 and 1968 respectively, came to nothing.

With assistance from South Africa and Portugal, Rhodesia defied international sanctions (the cutting of trade links to isolate the country economically). The possibility of black majority government was ruled out by the new constitution of 1969. This guaranteed white political supremacy.

The European population of 250,000 already had a monopoly of land. It had been allocated 272 million acres of (the best) land, the same area as that allocated to the black population of six million. The inevitable consequence was an outbreak of violence. For the next decade the conflict between black nationalists and the white administration escalated.

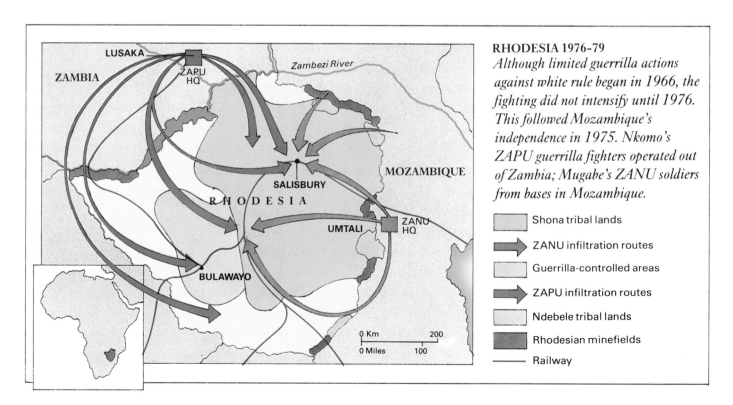

RHODESIA 1976-79
Although limited guerrilla actions against white rule began in 1966, the fighting did not intensify until 1976. This followed Mozambique's independence in 1975. Nkomo's ZAPU guerrilla fighters operated out of Zambia; Mugabe's ZANU soldiers from bases in Mozambique.

- Shona tribal lands
- ZANU infiltration routes
- Guerrilla-controlled areas
- ZAPU infiltration routes
- Ndebele tribal lands
- Rhodesian minefields
- Railway

Victorious guerrilla commanders, Zimbabwe, 1979.

The birth of Zimbabwe

From 1969 guerrilla groups conducted regular operations from sanctuaries (safe bases) in Zambia. Armed with Soviet rifles and landmines, the guerrillas attacked farmsteads, police posts and government buildings. Although these activities caused considerable disruption, it was the opening up of a new front in Mozambique which brought an entirely new dimension to the hostilities.

The end of Portuguese rule, and Mozambican independence in 1975, marked the beginning of the end for white Rhodesia. In the field the Rhodesian security forces were certainly effective. Highly mobile tactics, helicopter-borne commandos and the use of Special Forces achieved considerable success. South Africa also despatched contingents of paramilitary police to support Rhodesia's counterinsurgency offensive. But by the mid-1970s the Rhodesian forces were stretched to the limit.

The intensification of the guerrilla struggle from across the 1,100-km (700-mile) border with Mozambique led to a loss of morale among the whites. On top of this, South Africa's prime minister, John Vorster, had come to the conclusion that Smith's position was untenable. In his view, white rule in Rhodesia was doomed. Smith was pressurized in an effort to install a moderate black government in Rhodesia.

An Anglo-American plan in 1977 took the process one stage further. A program for the introduction of black majority rule, in which the interests of whites would be protected, was suggested. This included the proposal to merge the Rhodesian security forces and the guerrilla armies of the two major nationalist parties. However, the two black parties, Joshua Nkomo's Zimbabwe African People's Union (ZAPU) and Robert Mugabe's Zimbabwe African National Union (ZANU), were at loggerheads. The only thing they could agree on was their mutual dislike of Ian Smith.

As the negotiations foundered, the Rhodesian government decided to go for an "Internal Settlement" with Bishop Abel Muzorewa's moderate United African National Congress (UANC). A mixed white and black government came into being in June 1979 with Muzorewa as prime minister of Zimbabwe-Rhodesia.

However, this new regime was unacceptable to Nkomo and Mugabe. Their ZAPU and ZANU parties were now linked together in a loose alliance known as the Patriotic Front (PF). The guerrilla campaign was stepped up with a new sense of urgency, forcing Smith to begin negotiations afresh.

The British government played a major role in bringing the parties together and a ceasefire was arranged. Fresh elections were held in February 1980. Mugabe's ZANU won 57 of the 80 seats allocated to blacks. He became prime minister of an independent Zimbabwe in April 1980. Hemmed in by black countries to the north and the Atlantic and Indian oceans to the west and east, the Republic of South Africa remained the continent's final white redoubt.

Afrikaner supremacy

Until the mid-1970s, the South Africans regarded the territories of Angola, Mozambique and Rhodesia as a valuable buffer zone separating them from black Africa. However, the collapse of the Portuguese empire and the fall of the Smith regime removed this barrier. Macmillan's "Winds of Change" had finally reached the Republic of South Africa's own borders.

At South Africa's independence in 1910, the white settlers had complete control of the country. Many Afrikaners, however, wanted not only supremacy of white over black, but also Afrikaner over British. In the words of General James Hertzog, the founder of the National Party, "The Afrikaner must be master in South Africa."

In 1948 the National Party won a surprise electoral victory. This Afrikaner party has been in power ever since and has implemented a policy of apartheid. This racist strategy is the Afrikaner's blueprint for survival.

The black homelands

A succession of laws were passed to provide the framework for "Separate Development." The whole country was divided into areas. Only people of one specified race were to live in any given area. In this way Asians, coloreds (mixed race), blacks and whites were to live apart from each other. Between 1960 and 1972 over a million people were made to move into their specified areas. By mid-1982 the number had risen to 3.5 million. Within South Africa, 10 tribally-based African "Bantustans" (homelands) were established. Several of them (for example, Transkei, Ciskei, Venda) have been granted "independence." They have only been recognized by each other and by South Africa. The rest of the world regards them as illegal.

Through this policy of "divide and rule," the 4.8 million whites have been able to dominate a total population of 33 million. Blacks (numbering 24 million) are supposed to have their own form of political representation within their homelands. However, only

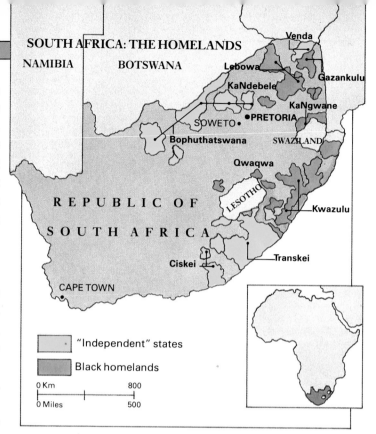

SOUTH AFRICA: THE HOMELANDS

NAMIBIA · BOTSWANA · Venda · Lebowa · KaNdebele · Gazankulu · KaNgwane · SOWETO · PRETORIA · Bophuthatswana · SWAZILAND · Qwaqwa · REPUBLIC OF SOUTH AFRICA · LESOTHO · Kwazulu · Ciskei · Transkei · CAPE TOWN

"Independent" states

Black homelands

0 Km — 800
0 Miles — 500

half the blacks live in their homelands. The other half live in "white areas" but are regarded as citizens of their language-group homelands. The white areas constitute more than 80 per cent of the country.

Those blacks living in workers' townships like Soweto (outside Johannesburg) represent something of a dilemma. On the one hand, they are essential to white prosperity; on the other, they pose a threat to white South African power.

Whites are represented in the House of Assembly. Since 1984, coloreds (2.8 million) have been represented in the House of Representatives and Indians (900,000) in the House of Delegates. In this fashion coloreds and Indians have been encouraged to join the white laager (fortress) against the threat of black majority rule. The aim has been to transform the political lineup from white versus non-white to non-black versus black.

Protecting the whites

In order to protect itself further, the South African regime has constructed a formidable security apparatus. Following the Sharpeville incident in March 1960, when 67 unarmed blacks were shot by police during a protest march – an action that aroused worldwide condemnation – black opposition went into exile or underground (setting up a secret organization). As this resistance became more violent, the security police became more expert. Today, it is one of the most effective secret police forces in the world.

At the same time, the South African Defense Force (SADF) has been built up into the most formidable war-machine in sub-Saharan Africa. Fully mobilized, it can muster more than 400,000 fighting men.

African opposition

On the other side, black nationalists also took to violence. The African National Congress (ANC) is the best known of their groups. One of its leaders, Nelson Mandela (known as "the black pimpernel" because he avoided arrest for so long), has been imprisoned since 1962. The ANC's military wing, *Umkhonto we Sizwe* ("Spear of the Nation"), was formed in 1961 by Nelson Mandela and other ANC militants.

Trained in a number of independent African states, it is dedicated to overthrowing apartheid. It has conducted guerrilla attacks on white economic and military targets such as an oil-from-coal installation in the Orange Free State in June 1980. Throughout the 1970s, there was a growth in black consciousness and thousands of young blacks joined the ANC following the 1976-77 Soweto riots, when schoolchildren fought the police. Black workers also became more militant and pressure on South African white rule intensified.

Present-day violence

South Africa entered the 1980s facing a deepening crisis. Rent increases in black townships sparked widespread rioting. Black policemen and community councillors accused of collaborating with the white authorities were attacked and killed. Despite the declaration of a State of Emergency, over 2,300 people died in the 1984-86 period. The majority were killed in security force operations, but black-on-black violence against those perceived as having a stake in the "system" accounted for over a third of these deaths.

President Botha's strategy of repression has been accompanied by statements on further reforms. The intention is to reach agreement with "responsible" black leaders – but not with the ANC. However, it seems clear that while Botha is interested in negotiations for sharing power, he is not interested in talks about a transfer of power.

Meanwhile, international efforts to force the pace of change through economic sanctions appear to have stiffened the whites' resolve. As Afrikanerdom withdraws into the laager, there is little prospect of a peaceful resolution to the crisis in this last bastion of white rule. The future does not look promising.

South African security guards break up a mob with batons, sjamboks *(whips) and dogs, Durban, 1986.*

Namibian independence

The Southwest Africa/Namibia issue is critically linked to the South African one. In 1919 the vast territory (824,000 sq km/318,000 square miles) was taken from Germany and handed over to be administered by South Africa until its people were ready for self-government. But South Africa has taken over the country entirely. The United Nations has tried to intervene to get "free" elections held but without success. South Africa's occupation is supported by Namibia's white population (ex-German settlers and Afrikaners), who number some 110,000, about 10 per cent of the total.

South Africa has defied international pressure because it does not want an independent radical Namibia on its doorstep. It also wants to retain control of Namibia's enormous mineral wealth (especially the diamond mines).

But since the late 1960s, the Southwest African People's Organization (SWAPO) has conducted a guerrilla campaign against South African rule. For the most part, its forces operate from bases in neighboring Angola. Since Angola's independence in 1975, SWAPO has become a greater threat. However, in both military and political terms, the Namibian issue appears to have entered a prolonged period of deadlock. At the present time, Namibia continues as a South African satellite, albeit with its own system of internal self-government.

Despite the speed with which the process of decolonization occurred, the problems of Africa were far from over. Quite often, the legacy of colonial rule was a cruel one, producing border disputes and internal rivalries that led to bitter conflict. As so many countries have discovered, independence is only the first step on a long road to peace and national identity.

South African troops search for SWAPO guerrillas in the war zone of northern Namibia, 1986.

AFRICA'S RESOURCES

AGRICULTURAL PRODUCE

- Cattle
- Sheep
- Cereals
- Grapes and wine
- Citrus fruits
- Cocoa
- Coffee
- Tea
- Tobacco
- Bananas
- Dates
- Palm Oil
- Natural rubber
- Sugar cane

MINERALS AND NATURAL RESOURCES

- Diamonds
- Gold
- Silver
- Copper
- Iron
- Lead
- Phosphates
- Tin
- Zinc
- Bauxite
- Oil
- Natural Gas
- Coal
- Uranium
- Alloy metals (manganese, chromium, tungsten, etc)

CHAPTER 3
INDEPENDENT AFRICA

Independent Africa has faced a multitude of problems, many of which, responding to the pressures created by decolonization, have resulted in armed conflict. Military coups have introduced a tradition of political violence to many countries, while tribal loyalties, existing in opposition to those demanded by the state, have led to bitter internal wars. Finally, border disputes – an inevitable legacy of imposed colonial rule – have caused friction and wars between individual countries.

Since the end of the Second World War, almost 50 African countries have become independent. During this brief period, the African peoples found the means to end European rule in most of the continent. Yet despite the unparalleled speed with which the emancipation from foreign occupation occurred, there are still many reminders of the years of colonial rule.

Borders drawn up by the imperial powers remained intact at independence. The colonies have become states. But the boundaries which had been mapped out by the Europeans were essentially artificial. Roughly speaking, there are some 1,200 societies or major tribal groupings in Africa. These groups were either divided between colonial territories (for example, the Ewes were split between Ghana and Togo) or arbitrarily grouped into larger ones (such as Angola).

Communities that had no common history before the arrival of European conquerors – or that had been traditionally hostile to each other – found themselves citizens of the same country. Hausas, Ibos and Yorubas became Nigerians; Ndebele and Shona shared a new nationality as Zimbabweans. Thus throughout Africa it is very rare indeed for the modern country to be made up of an individual society. Most Africans are more conscious of ethnic loyalties than of national ones. This makes it very difficult to forge such states into unified bodies with a true sense of identity. With only a few exceptions, both domestic politics and relationships between neighboring countries have been strongly influenced by tribal or ethnic antagonisms. This has resulted in wide-scale civil and military conflicts.

Economic problems

Another difficulty is that the vast majority of African countries are economically weak. The African continent is the most impoverished region of the world. At independence, most of the population were peasant farmers. For the majority of these, life was a constant struggle. Educational and health facilities were also extremely limited. For instance, by the time Malawi gained its freedom it had only two secondary schools for its population of 3 million; the former Belgian Congo, ten times the size of West Germany, had 13 university graduates. Death rates for children were the highest in the world and life expectancy was the lowest. Even today most males in Mali die before they reach the age of 30.

It is true that parts of the continent have rich mineral resources (Angola, Algeria and Gabon, for example, have vast oil reserves), but most countries are heavily dependent on just one or two primary products. Zambia and Zanzibar depend for more than 90 per cent of their income on, respectively, copper and cloves. They are highly vulnerable to price changes on the international market. If the price goes down, their economies go into steep decline.

Political problems

A third general problem facing independent Africa is that its new rulers were unsure of themselves and inexperienced. They also had to find suitable political institutions for their countries. Most African states inherited constitutions modeled on the system of the ex-colonial power. Kenya and Uganda were provided with the "Westminster" model of Britain, that is, one in which two main political parties representing opposing policies fight elections in order to gain the right to run the country.

The constitutions of the Ivory Coast and Senegal were modeled on France's Fifth Republic. This is a system headed by a president, where there are many parties who receive the number of seats according to the proportion of votes obtained in an election.

After the departure of the European authorities, multi-party politics quickly gave way to the one-party state. Faced with illiterate populations, grave economic problems and ethnic rivalries, most of the new African leaders maintained that parliamentary democracy was an expensive luxury that the continent could ill afford. Party conflicts and frequent changes of government were too costly. Multi-party systems undermined national unity and could be dangerous. All efforts, they argued, had to be mobilized for the task of nation-building. A one-party system would eliminate wasteful squabblings, bringing unity and cohesion in its wake.

One-party systems

Thus, political elites that had won elections at independence soon set about eliminating their rivals. Opposition parties, many of which were ethnically based, were banned. Many of their leaders were persecuted and imprisoned. Others "crossed the floor" and joined the government party. Most leaders abandoned the political systems they had inherited, partly for reasons of ambition and selfishness, and partly because of the many problems facing their countries.

Most of the one-party states were established under the personal rule of one man. Presidentialism – the concentration of power in the hands of a single figure – became commonplace throughout Africa: Nkrumah in Ghana, Omar Bongo in Gabon, Touré in Guinea. Several of these leaders permitted a degree of freedom within the single party; others became brutal dictators.

Some African states have remained under the guidance of the men who first led them to independence: Banda in Malawi, Kaunda in Zambia and Houphouët-Boigny in the Ivory Coast. Others, like Equatorial Guinea or Uganda, fell under the yokes of monstrous tyrants (Macias Nguema, Idi Amin), whose names became bywords for horrific repression.

In many cases, however, the abolition of legal ways of organizing opposition means that the only way to unseat presidents and prime ministers is to use violence. Military *coups d'état* (where the armed forces seize power), not elections, have become the chief method of changing governments.

MILITARY COUPS

At first, no one realized that the African armed forces would play a key role in the newly independent African countries. But since the 1960s, there has been a rash of military interventions. Rapid officer Africanization (the replacement of whites by Africans), the weakness of civilian (non-military) institutions, personal ambitions, political corruption and economic crises all help to explain the number of *coups d'état*.

Although there had already been a number of *coups d'état* in Egypt (1952), the Sudan (1958) and the Congo (1960), the main sequence began in Togo in 1963 when President Sylvanus Olympio was assassinated by army rebels. A new government was installed under the civilian President Nicholas Grunitzky, but he was in turn overthrown by Colonel Étienne Eyadema on the fourth anniversary of Olympio's murder. Eyadema has been in power ever since.

Following the great wave of independence that traversed Africa in the years 1960-63, military coups swept through the continent. There were four coups in 1965; the next year there were six, two within the space of six months in Nigeria. By 1972, Dahomey (later Benin) had seen no less than five *coups d'état*. This record is now equaled by Ghana.

Thirty-one African states have already experienced successful coups and 16 have had more than one. On top of this, there have been countless attempted coups. For every successful coup in Africa there have been at least two unsuccessful ones. At the beginning of 1987, half the continent's countries were under military rule – in many cases for the second or third time. Some of them (for instance, Nigeria, the Sudan, Libya) have been under military government for most of their independent existence.

The majority of coups have been against civilian regimes. An increasing proportion, however, are staged from within the military, by one clique of soldiers against another – as occurred in Ghana in July 1978 and again in June 1979. To begin with military coups were led by generals and colonels. More recently, *coups d'état* have been staged by the junior ranks. Flight-Lieutenant Jerry Rawlings led two coups in Ghana.

Ghana's military ruler, Jerry Rawlings, 1982.

In 1980 Master-Sergeant Samuel Doe put a bloody end to President William Tolbert's civilian regime in Liberia. On that occasion, Doe and his accomplices burst into the Presidential palace and killed Tolbert in his bedroom. His body was dumped in a mass grave together with 27 others who died defending the palace. The ruthlessness of the coup was underlined by the revenge executions of 13 more ministers and officials.

Another surprising feature is that military coups have usually involved only a few hundred troops. In Ghana, the National Liberation Council, composed of army and police officers, came into power in February 1966 when 500 soldiers, from an army of 10,000, toppled the regime of Dr Nkrumah. In the Congo (now Zaire), Colonel Sese Seko Mobutu "neutralized" the conflict between Prime Minister Lumumba and President Kasavubu by seizing the capital, Léopoldville (now Kinshasa), with 200 men in September 1960. Even more extraordinary was the case of General Christophe Soglo in Dahomey. In December 1967, he was removed from office by just 60 paratroopers.

The mechanics of a coup

How are such actions possible? There are two answers to this question. On the one hand, the soldiers have a virtual monopoly over the arms which are used to intimidate civilians, for example, rifles, armored vehicles and other equipment. They are also relatively well-disciplined and self-sufficient. Civilian groups are by contrast weak, divided and ineffective. On the other hand, the concentration in the capital of the state's major institutions and personalities makes a military rebellion quite simple. Once a few key individuals and places have been seized (government ministers, the Presidential palace, radio and television stations and airports), the success of the coup is virtually assured.

Nevertheless, the opportunity and means to seize office violently do not explain why soldiers actually do so. In justifying their actions, the soldiers blame the corruption and mismanagement of the previous civilian administration. There are four broad types of military intervention.

Four types of coups

The "security coup" is undertaken to replace a regime judged incapable of defending the state from internal challenges. As with the January 1966 coup in Nigeria, the primary aim is to restore law and order.

Second, military intervention may be prompted by a dissatisfaction with the character or policies of the regime. This is the "reform coup," the objective of which is the reform of domestic or foreign policy. For instance, Colonel Muammar Gaddafi's seizure of power in Libya in 1969 was designed to usher in an Islamic socialist society.

The "punitive coup," the third type, occurs when there are grievances within the armed forces against a regime which is accused of undermining the position or prestige of the military. Colonel Ignatius Acheampong's 1972 Ghana *coup d'état* against Dr Kofi Busia is a prime example. It seems to have been staged to restore cuts in officers' salaries and benefits. Indeed, Busia called it "an officers' amenities coup." After the coup, the military budget increased substantially.

This leads to the fourth type, the "new elite coup," motivated primarily by ambitious and power-hungry men who use the army to seize political office for their own ends. This type of coup is frequently linked to regional rivalries. Colonel Taya's 1984 coup in Mauritania fits into this final type. But in nearly all cases, coups are staged for a combination of reasons.

Military rule

In political terms, military administrations range from the pro-West and conservative ones of Zaire, Guinea and Lesotho, through the mildly socialist examples of Burundi and Liberia, to the Marxist and pro-Soviet regimes of Colonel Mengistu Haile Mariam's Ethiopia and Colonel Mathieu Kerekou's Benin.

Having seized office, the armed forces have not been especially keen to withdraw. "Dawn broadcasts," announcing the coups by radio or television, invariably state that the imposition of military rule will be a short-term affair. The action is presented as a temporary or interim measure. Even General Amin, who seized power in Uganda from President Milton Obote in January 1971, gave the same assurances. His regime lasted eight years.

By criticizing the civilian politicians, the soldiers justify their intervention in the political arena. They present themselves as untainted guardians of the people and saviors of the nation. The military takeover is often welcomed by the people.

However, the honeymoon period is usually short-lived. The truth of the saying "power corrupts, and absolute power corrupts absolutely" is frequently revealed in military regimes. Like the politicians before them, officers quickly acquire a taste for the trappings of high office: fine mansions, state banquets, foreign travel, status and prestige.

Abuses of power

Thus the decadence and corruption of the civilian politicians tend to be reproduced within the ranks of the military. The manipulation of office to gain wealth reached outrageous proportions in the person of Colonel Jean-Bédel Bokassa of the Central African Republic, which he declared an empire. After seizing power on New Year's Day 1966, he had himself crowned emperor in a lavish $18 million Napoleonic-style coronation 11 years later. The cost was the equivalent of a quarter of his country's annual national revenue.

Military rule in Africa has been noted not only for its excesses, but also for its inadequacies. Neither Ghana's five military administrations nor Nigeria's four have put an end to corruption or economic decline. In many states, military rule has often been a good deal harsher than civilian rule. Some military regimes became notorious for their sheer brutality.

The tyranny of President Nguema in Equatorial Guinea reached appalling proportions in the 1970s.

Left: Bokassa's lavish coronation, 1977.
Below: Students protest against Ethiopia's government in the build-up to the military coup, 1974.

Having forced his way to power in 1968, Nguema, a member of the Fang tribe, virtually turned his tiny country into a concentration camp. Numerous reports from exiles and Amnesty International told blood-chilling stories of slow death by starvation and disease and hideous tortures. The use of young girls as slave labor was also a hallmark of Nguema's regime.

By the time of Colonel Teodoro Mbasogo's coup in 1979, Nguema's 11 years of rule had resulted in 43,000 deaths. At least one quarter of the country's 350,000 population was in exile. Only two doctors remained in the country, one of whom, a psychiatrist, was employed to treat Nguema for an assortment of mental disorders. After the coup, Nguema was put on trial and executed.

Ousting the military

Once the army has intervened in politics, however, it is very difficult for it to return to barracks. Each coup exposes the armed forces to new political demands and pressures. As long as the military remains outside politics, it can maintain a sense of unity. But once the soldiers seize office, civilian groups seek alliances with different military factions. Society's wider divisions – regional, religious and political – penetrate the ranks of the military.

As a result, all military "juntas" (governments) constantly live under the threat of a countercoup by disgruntled or ambitious soldiers, or by a combination of soldiers and civilians. Thus, rather than resolving domestic conflict, military intervention has contributed to the pattern of lasting political instability in numerous African states.

WARS OF SECESSION

It has been argued that in many cases the transition from colonial dependency to sovereign state was too abrupt, sometimes provoking a war of secession. This occurs when a discontented group tries to establish a new breakaway country.

In Western Sahara, for example, the colonial power, Spain, left without having organized a proper transfer of power to local politicians. Morocco and Mauritania occupied the phosphate-rich territory, claiming it in terms of their "historic rights." A nationalist movement, POLISARIO, forced the Mauritanians out of the country in 1979. But the conflict between POLISARIO and Morocco continues to this day.

For three of Africa's largest states, Nigeria, the Sudan and Ethiopia, independence ushered in serious outbreaks of civil strife. In the Congo, the province of Katanga attempted to assert its independence. This sparked off a series of rebellions in the country.

The Congo

The rapid transformation from Belgian colony to independent republic on June 30, 1960, threw the Congo into chaos. Within five days, army (*Force Publique*) units had mutinied and anti-white violence broke out. These attacks resulted in a mass exodus of Europeans, and the Belgian government had to send 5,000 paratroops into the country to protect Belgian nationals.

At the same time the southern copper-rich province of Katanga announced its independence as Shaba under Moise Tshombe. Backed by Belgian business interests and white mercenaries (foreign soldiers who are paid to fight), Tshombe saw no reason why his wealthy province's revenues and taxes should go to the central government in Léopoldville.

Following this disastrous start to independence, President Kasavubu requested United Nations' (UN) assistance to put down the secession and expel the Belgian troops. He could not use his own army since it was in a state of mutiny. In January 1963, Tshombe abandoned his claim that Katanga should be independent and, by the end of 1963, UN soldiers had managed to restore order.

The breakdown of civilian rule

Meanwhile the confusion was made worse when Kasavubu and his prime minister, Lumumba, quarreled about who should run the government. After trying to dismiss each other, both were dismissed in 1960 by Colonel Mobutu, the army commander, in a *coup d'état*. Lumumba escaped, was recaptured by Congolese soldiers and taken to Katanga, where in 1961 he was killed in mysterious circumstances.

Mobutu restored civilian rule with Kasavubu as president and Cyrille Adoula as prime minister but Lumumba's supporters, now led by Antoine Gizenga, attempted to form a government of their own in Stanleyville (Kisangani). For a while they were supported by the Soviets, who resented Western influence in the Congo. Negotiations led to a compromise, but genuine reconciliation in the country was not reached until 1964 when Tshombe was invited by Kasavubu to become prime minister, and accepted.

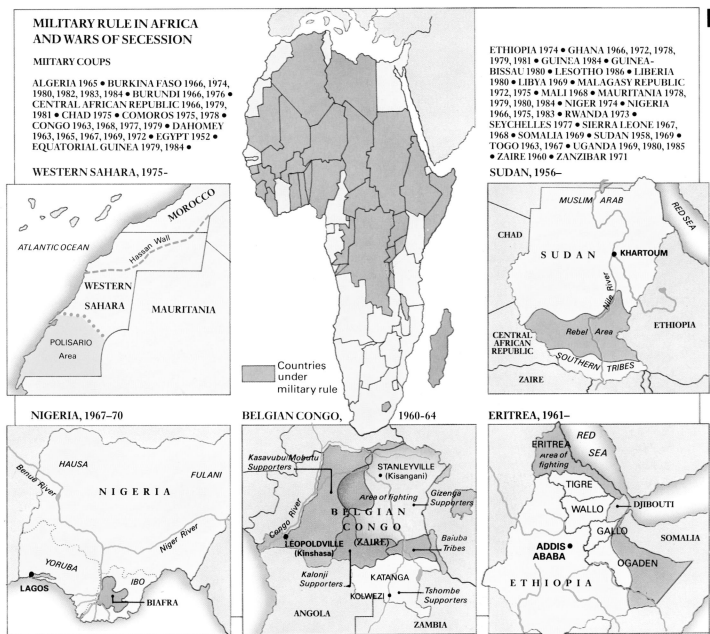

MILITARY RULE IN AFRICA AND WARS OF SECESSION

MILITARY COUPS

ALGERIA 1965 • BURKINA FASO 1966, 1974, 1980, 1982, 1983, 1984 • BURUNDI 1966, 1976 • CENTRAL AFRICAN REPUBLIC 1966, 1979, 1981 • CHAD 1975 • COMOROS 1975, 1978 • CONGO 1963, 1968, 1977, 1979 • DAHOMEY 1963, 1965, 1967, 1969, 1972 • EGYPT 1952 • EQUATORIAL GUINEA 1979, 1984 •

ETHIOPIA 1974 • GHANA 1966, 1972, 1978, 1979, 1981 • GUINEA 1984 • GUINEA-BISSAU 1980 • LESOTHO 1986 • LIBERIA 1980 • LIBYA 1969 • MALAGASY REPUBLIC 1972, 1975 • MALI 1968 • MAURITANIA 1978, 1979, 1980, 1984 • NIGER 1974 • NIGERIA 1966, 1975, 1983 • RWANDA 1973 • SEYCHELLES 1977 • SIERRA LEONE 1967, 1968 • SOMALIA 1969 • SUDAN 1958, 1969 • TOGO 1963, 1967 • UGANDA 1969, 1980, 1985 • ZAIRE 1960 • ZANZIBAR 1971

Countries under military rule

WESTERN SAHARA, 1975–

ATLANTIC OCEAN
MOROCCO
Hassan Wall
WESTERN SAHARA
MAURITANIA
POLISARIO Area

SUDAN, 1956–

MUSLIM ARAB
RED SEA
CHAD
SUDAN • KHARTOUM
Nile River
CENTRAL AFRICAN REPUBLIC
Rebel Area
ETHIOPIA
SOUTHERN TRIBES
ZAIRE

NIGERIA, 1967–70

Benue River
HAUSA
FULANI
NIGERIA
Niger River
YORUBA
IBO
LAGOS
BIAFRA

BELGIAN CONGO, 1960–64

Kasavubu/Mobutu Supporters
STANLEYVILLE (Kisangani)
Area of fighting
Gizenga Supporters
BELGIAN CONGO (ZAIRE)
Congo River
LÉOPOLDVILLE (Kinshasa)
Baiuba Tribes
Kalonji Supporters
KATANGA
KOLWEZI
Tshombe Supporters
ANGOLA
ZAMBIA

ERITREA, 1961–

ERITREA Area of fighting
RED SEA
TIGRE
WALLO
DJIBOUTI
GALLO
ADDIS ABABA
SOMALIA
OGADEN
ETHIOPIA

In 1964, after the UN forces had withdrawn, a new rebellion in Stanleyville led to Belgian military intervention to rescue hostages. Back in Léopoldville, a new struggle for political power ended in a bloodless coup in 1965. General Mobutu suspended all political activity, proclaimed himself president and instituted a harsh regime which provided the Congo with a degree of stability.

However, in 1977, exiled Katangans invaded Shaba from Angola and were repulsed by Franco-Moroccan military forces. The invasion was repeated in 1978, Kolwezi was captured and again France intervened, this time with Belgian assistance. On both occasions, foreign troops were flown in at Mobutu's request. Since then, Shaba has been comparatively quiet, but the potential for further trouble persists.

The Sudan

At independence on January 1, 1956, the most profound division within Sudanese society was that between the 3.5 million southern tribes and the more prosperous 8 million Muslim Arabs of the north. The problems between the two started in the 19th century when the Arab traders raided the south for slaves. In 1955, even before independence, southern soldiers had revolted against their Arab officers. It was a bloody affair and government reprisals were even bloodier as 8,000 troops were sent from the north.

For most of the period since 1956, the southerners have been more or less in open rebellion. They have attempted to gain either a federal constitution or the establishment of a separate country. To date, they have been unsuccessful.

In 1958, General Ibrahim Abboud decided that the southern problem should be overcome decisively. He staged a military coup to end what he called "a state of degeneration, chaos and instability." His tough action was resisted by a number of groups, which joined together in 1963 to form the "Anya Nya" Liberation Movement, derived from words meaning "snake venom." For the next decade, the secessionist struggle claimed hundreds of thousands of lives. It was fought with a high degree of ruthlessness in which neither side took prisoners.

A complete breakdown of government authority in the south led to a second *coup d'état*, staged by General Gaafar Mohammed Nimeiri in 1969. He continued to prosecute the war vigorously. However, recognizing the need for a political solution, he initiated peace talks in 1972 that led to a limited degree of local autonomy (self-rule) in the south.

In 1983, however, anti-government activities in Africa's largest country broke out anew. This time they were led by the rebel Sudanese People's Liberation Army, under the leadership of Colonel John Garang. Demanding a greater southern share in the central government, he operates from the Ethiopian capital of Addis Ababa as a guest of Colonel Mengistu's Marxist regime. In retaliation, the Sudan is backing Eritrean rebels fighting for secession from Ethiopia.

Eritrea

Ethiopia, which has an area of over 1 million sq km (nearly 400,000 square miles), harbors several secessionist civil wars. The best-known of them is in Eritrea (meaning "Red Sea"), a former Italian territory. It was administered by Britain from 1941 to 1952, when it was handed over to Ethiopia, as decided by the United Nations. A federal constitution was introduced which allowed Eritrea a large degree of autonomy. But in 1962, amid allegations of bribery, harassment and corruption, the Eritrean assembly voted for full union with Ethiopia.

Women freedom fighters undergoing training in Ethiopia's war-torn Tigre province.

This decision was challenged by Eritrean nationalists, who had established the Eritrean Liberation Front (ELF) in 1961 to forestall Ethiopian "imperialism." It received immediate support from Arab states sympathetic to Eritrea's Muslim majority. The central government regards the rebellion as a secessionist war which, if successful, would leave Ethiopia as Africa's 15th landlocked state. By contrast, the Eritreans claim independence and do not regard their land as belonging to Ethiopia.

A series of successful hijackings in 1969 won the ELF considerable publicity, but it was challenged by the more radical Eritrean People's Liberation Front (EPLF). Little headway was made until 1975, when the Eritrean guerrillas almost succeeded in capturing the Eritrean capital, Asmara. This and other successes won concessions from the ruling Dergue (military committee), which had ousted Emperor Haile Selassie's regime by a coup in 1974. The Dergue offered Eritrea self-rule in 1977, but the rebels refused to accept anything less than total independence.

This proved to be a mistake. With the assistance of Cuban and Soviet forces, the Dergue intensified its anti-rebel war in the province. The ruthless assaults, which involved 100,000 government troops and included random bombing of civilian targets, reduced separatist control to the countryside.

Nevertheless, the viciousness of the Ethiopian regime drove thousands of recruits into the arms of the ELF and the EPLF. By the end of 1986, the rebels' tactics of a protracted people's war showed no signs of weakening. Elsewhere in Ethiopia, similar but smaller insurrections continued in Tigre, Gallo, Ogaden, and against the Omoro and Afars.

Nigeria

Within seven years of independence, on October 1, 1960, Nigeria was engulfed in a secessionist war that was one of the bloodiest conflicts in modern African history. Africa's most populous country is split up into three regionally dominant groups: the Hausa in the north, the Yoruba in the west and the Ibo in the east. To all intents and purposes these peoples were separate nations, divided by language, culture and mutual suspicions. The northern peoples, who were predominantly Muslim, were believed to outnumber the other two non-Muslim peoples.

At independence, the federal government was a coalition between the north and the east. The western leader, Chief Obafemi Awolowo, formed an opposition party in the federal parliament.

However, the accord between north and east soon broke down. The tie was finally severed in 1964 when the Ibo party attempted to win parliamentary seats in the north where a large community of Ibos lived. Meanwhile the eastern region was encouraged to oppose northern domination by its growing oil production. Transparently dishonest elections in 1965 led to a pro-Ibo army *coup d'état* in January 1966. It was a demonstration against northern rule and corrupt government. The federal prime minister, Sir Abubakar Tafawa Balewa, a wise and moderate statesman, was murdered along with many other politicians.

The installation of a new Ibo military leader, General Aguiyi Ironsi, prompted northern fears of eastern dominance. After anti-Ibo riots in the north, this flared up in another coup and Ironsi was murdered by northern officers. The army was divided. General Yakubu Gowon, a northern Christian, eventually assumed full control in July 1966, but he was unable to stop savage massacres of Ibos living in the north.

Refugees flee to Sudan from Tigre province.

In retaliation, Ibos killed Hausas resident in the east. These attacks continued until all Ibos had fled from the north and all Hausas from the east. Two million refugees escaped to the security of their own regions. The Ibos' distrust of Hausa supremacy, and their fears that they would always be downtrodden in a united Nigeria, were now overwhelming. Under the leadership of Colonel Odumegwu Ojukwu, the Ibo east decided to declare itself the independent state of Biafra in July 1967.

During the bloody two-and-a-half-year war that followed, Biafra received encouragement from several countries, including France and Zambia. However, almost all the Organization of African Unity (OAU) states backed Gowon's federal forces. Both Britain and the Soviet Union supplied arms to the Nigerian government. Because Biafra received outside assistance, the federal forces were not able to end the revolt quickly. It has been estimated that 600,000 lives were lost as Biafra struggled against overwhelming odds. Eventually lack of supplies, starvation and disease forced the Ibos to surrender in January 1970.

CIVIL WARS

Despite obvious similarities, not all civil wars involve secessionist demands. Such wars are frequently fought not to split up the country but to decide who should run it. This section deals with a number of cases where civil wars have been waged as a result of rivalry for power within the state. In all three conflicts examined here, the wars have been fought because of the unwillingness of large sectors of the population to submit to the authority of the state.

For a variety of ethnic, regional and ideological (differing political ideas) reasons, the peoples of several African states have set upon one another. Two of the best known are the civil wars in the former Portuguese colonies of Angola and Mozambique. A third civil war has long engulfed the huge landlocked territory of Chad. But these have not been the only uprisings against ruling regimes. In a host of lesser revolts, violent challenges to African governments have also occurred in Cameroun (1961-72), Rwanda (1963-64), Burundi (1964) and Uganda (1966). Small though these countries are, the violence in Rwanda and Burundi was intense, with large numbers of people being killed.

Chad

Completely surrounded by six African states, with Libya to the north and Nigeria to the southwest, Chad has one of the lowest *per capita* incomes (the average amount earned in any one year by a single person) in the world. Independence from France under the presidency of François Tombalbaye came in August 1960. He immediately set about consolidating his personal power, banning all parties in 1962 except his own. He became a dictator who relied on the non-Muslim population of the south.

Not surprisingly, Tombalbaye's single-party policy was opposed by the Muslim politicians of the north. In 1963 anti-government riots took place in the capital, N'Djamena. These were brutally suppressed and 500 people died. By 1965 a rebellion that had begun in the northern half of Chad had escalated into a full-scale civil war. A major source of grievance was the imposition of tax levies in the north. With the Muslim-dominated Sudanese government's assistance, the Chad National Liberation Front (FROLINAT) was established in 1966. Tombalbaye's regime only survived through French intervention in 1971.

A *coup d'état* overthrew and killed Tombalbaye in April 1975. However, the new Supreme Military Council headed by General Félix Malloum continued to be opposed by FROLINAT. With support from Libya's Gaddafi, the guerrillas gained control of northern Chad by 1978. To counter Libyan ambitions in Chad, the French intervened to save Malloum; but in 1980, 14,000 Libyan soldiers seized N'Djamena and announced the "union" of Libya with Chad.

Gaddafi soon managed to upset those who had originally welcomed Libyan support. As a result, the Libyans were forced to fall back to northernmost Chad. There they installed a rival government in the Aozou Strip. This uranium-rich territory had been annexed by Libya some years earlier.

By 1983, two men were claiming to be president of Chad. With funding from the United States, President Hissène Habré's army occupied N'Djamena; meanwhile, "President" Goukouni Oueddei's forces, supported by Libya, occupied northern Chad and advanced on the capital. Once again French troops, supported by Jaguar fighter-planes, were airlifted to Chad. France acted as a buffer between the rival factions, and resumed its role of policing Chad. Although Gaddafi's forces suffered major defeats in 1987, there is still no sign of any settlement of this desert strife.

Angola

In November 1975, after 400 years of Portuguese colonial occupation, Angola followed the path of Guinea-Bissau and Mozambique into formal independence. But the celebrations of newly-acquired statehood were soured by a civil war, which like the Sudanese one, began even before independence had been achieved. Freedom from foreign rule left three rival liberation groups vying for power: Holden Roberto's FNLA, Jonas Savimbi's UNITA (supported in the south by the Ovimbundu), and the MPLA, which seized power at independence. Angola has been in a state of civil war ever since.

The MPLA regime was only able to resist early FNLA/UNITA advances on its urban strongholds because of Soviet and Cuban assistance. Initially the FNLA enjoyed backing from Zaire and the United States, but it was soon repulsed by government forces. Savimbi's pro-West rebels have conducted a relentless campaign, forcing the government to commit half its national budget to defense. In this, UNITA has been aided by South Africa as well as the United States. South Africa maintains that UNITA represents the majority of Angolans. Accordingly, UNITA has received large-scale South African aid.

Angola's consistent support for the attempts of the Southwest Africa People's Organization (SWAPO) to win independence for Namibia explains South Africa's involvement. It has given the excuse the South Africans need to mount military missions against Angola on the grounds that it is pursuing SWAPO "terrorists" into their Angolan sanctuaries. Since 1975 South African forces have occupied large areas of Angola on various occasions. However, the presence of some 30,000 Cuban troops and Soviet "advisers" in support of the MPLA has resulted in tough military counter-measures. Yet to date, at least, these forces have been insufficient to rout UNITA guerrillas or South African ground troops.

Meanwhile, as long as UNITA can present itself as a genuine alternative to the Angolan government, South Africa will continue to justify its intervention. A stalemate exists in which the struggle for power between competing Angolan factions is complicated by outside involvement. Because Angola is potentially rich and strategically located, it will not be left to determine its own future. As with the Biafran episode and the Congo bloodbath, the Angolan civil war has never been just a national conflict but an international one.

The civil war in Chad has continued since 1965. Here anti-government guerrillas display their weaponry.

Mozambique

With a population of 12.5 million, Mozambique has been run by a single party since independence in 1975. This is FRELIMO, headed by President Machel until his death in a plane crash in October 1986. In 1975, South Africa's then prime minister, Vorster, accepted the Portuguese departure from the territory and continued to maintain close economic relations with Mozambique. However, African National Congress (ANC) insurgents began to use Mozambique as a major base from which to launch guerrilla attacks against apartheid. A chill crept into Mozambican-South African relations.

To thwart the ANC threat, South Africa began to provide massive military assistance to the Mozambique National Resistance (MNR). The pro-West MNR had emerged in the late 1970s as a major opponent to Machel's regime. Operating in bands of 100-200, the MNR has wreaked havoc throughout much of the country and left the economy in ruins.

Reeling under the crippling impact of the civil war, drought and famine, President Machel signed the Nkomati nonaggression pact with South Africa in March 1984. Mozambique expelled the ANC guerrillas from its soil; on its part, South Africa agreed to end its aid to Mozambique's rebels.

Just before the signing, however, South Africa organized a large resupply program to the MNR. Claiming that there were still ANC guerrillas in

FRELIMO troops inspect MNR sabotage, 1986.

Mozambique, South Africa continued to "destabilize" its neighbor through assistance to the MNR. Far from bringing peace, Nkomati brought a wider war.

BORDER DISPUTES

To a great extent, the political map of 1914 colonial Africa saw very little subsequent change. Within half a century, the colonial boundaries became the basis for the territorial division of independent Africa. The permanence of these borders was reinforced when the Organization of African Unity (OAU) was born in Addis Ababa in May 1963. The OAU is a league of African states dedicated to achieving cooperation between its members.

Declaring that they would settle their differences by conciliation and mediation within the African community, the member states pledged themselves to observe one another's political and territorial integrity. On the whole, the OAU countries have attempted to discourage forceful secessions and attempts to alter the present frontiers. The organization believes that, although the borders cut across many ethnic areas and enclose other groups unwillingly together, failure to uphold them would result in never-ending conflict.

But what the OAU stands for in principle does not always match up to what its members actually do. Since independence, African countries have clashed with each other militarily on dozens of occasions. Most of these hostilities have involved border disputes, but interstate aggression has sometimes reached right across the continent. Two of the largest-scale issues concern hostilities between Ethiopia and Somalia, and between Tanzania and Uganda.

War in the Ogaden

In comparison with most of Africa's states, Somalia is almost unique; it is a country based on one people. But there were 1 million Somalis living in the Ogaden region of southeast Ethiopia, 200,000 in northern Kenya and 40,000 in Djibouti. This was yet another example of how the partition of Africa had divided nations between different countries.

The unification of all the Somali peoples has been the declared objective of every Somali government since 1960. However, the situation has been complicated by the intensification of external involvement in the Horn of Africa – a region of crucial strategic significance for both major superpowers, since it controls access to the Red Sea. Between them, the United States and the Soviet Union have armed Ethiopia and Somalia with modern weapons.

The quarrel between Ethiopia and Somalia developed into full-scale war in 1977 when General Siad Barre, who had seized power in Somalia in 1969, took advantage of political upheavals in Ethiopia to overrun most of the Ogaden. The Western Somali Liberation Front (WSLF) aimed at nothing less than the joining of the Ogaden to Somalia. In this they were backed by Somali troops. Their success was short-lived, for in 1978 the Ethiopian army – backed by vast quantities of Soviet equipment and 12,000 Cuban troops – inflicted a crushing blow on the Somalis at Jijiga.

Sporadic fighting in the region has continued but Ethiopia's military superiority, together with a series of devastating droughts in the Ogaden, has cooled Somalia's ambitions.

Somali tribesmen in the Ogaden, 1977.

Tanzania invades Uganda

Idi Amin Dada's 1971 coup plunged Uganda into an eight-year nightmare. The Amin era became infamous for political repression, violence and bloodshed. To maintain his grip, Amin used terror. His army units and the State Research Bureau were responsible for up to 270,000 deaths.

Within a six-week period in 1972, 400,000 Ugandan Asians were expelled from the country. With them went the business skills so important to the developing world. Relations with Tanzania reached an all-time low. The reason for this was that Tanzania's President Julius Nyerere was a close friend of the man Amin had deposed, Dr Milton Obote.

In September 1972, Obote supporters, with Nyerere's help, invaded Uganda from Tanzania. They were decisively repulsed and Ugandan bombers attacked Bukoba in Tanzania.

In 1978, in an attempt to distract growing internal and especially army opposition to his regime, Amin launched a new attack on the Kagera Salient of northern Tanzania. In 1979, a 35,000-strong Tanzanian force invaded Uganda, seized the capital Kampala, and forced Amin into exile. Obote eventually emerged as president, but the brutal excesses of his own regime led to two further military takeovers.

Almost without exception, therefore, Africa's fledgling countries have faced a host of deep-seated conflicts. While many of these were political, their underlying causes were dictated by the region's economic conditions, creating pressures which few governments have been unable to escape.

An irrigation project in Burkina Faso.

CHAPTER 4
AN UNCERTAIN FUTURE

The future of large parts of Africa seems bleak. Even without the violence of coups and wars, vast numbers of people face economic problems which seem impossible to solve. A rapid growth in population has led to shortages of food, producing starvation and disease; governments have borrowed money to ease the burden, only to enter a situation of endless, growing debt. Foreign aid can help, but only if channeled toward development rather than dependence

In order to understand Africa's current condition and future prospects, one has to look at its history. The partition of Africa at the turn of the century left behind a welter of unresolved issues. In their eagerness to parcel out the spoils, the European powers drew up artificial boundaries, dividing tribes, language groups and communities. There are some 130 international frontiers in Africa and it was these that formed the basis of independence when the Europeans departed.

The colonial legacy

Fragmented into 50 or so territorial units, independent Africa has inherited an enduring European legacy: the nation-state. But there is little relation between nationhood and statehood. It is this tension that has produced the conflicts of modern Africa. The upheavals of the last two decades have their roots in a combination of economic, climatic, ideological and ethnic circumstances.

These have been described by one Nigerian professor, Adelbaya Adedji, as the "Seven Ds" – drought, desertification (the spread of desert regions), demography, dependency, disequilibrium, destabilization and debt. They have affected the lives and livelihoods of the majority of Africa's 500 million population. The continent is the home of numerous refugees, more than 10 million of whom have been driven into exile through civil and interstate wars, political and religious persecution, social upheavals and natural disaster, especially famine and drought. The refugee situation worsens as new crises emerge, or as existing ones escalate.

Poverty and population growth

Africa is also grappling with the ravages of poverty, overpopulation and disease. Dietary deficiencies and poor sanitation are closely related to the high incidence of endemic sicknesses. These include cholera, diphtheria, leprosy, bubonic plague, yellow fever and *kwashiorkor* (a children's nutritional disease due to protein deficiency).

Malarial parasites transmitted by mosquitoes account for a million infant and child deaths each year. More recently, the killer-disease AIDS has spread rapidly through central Africa. Combating such afflictions has become vital to the fight against poverty and deprivation.

The impact of such scourges is magnified by the fact that, despite containing two dozen of the earth's 38 poorest countries, the continent confronts the world's fastest population growth. Africa does not lack the basic resources to feed itself; the 39 states south of the Sahara have a fifth of the planet's cultivable land and only 9 per cent of its people.

Yet their ability to struggle up the development ladder, out of existing or threatened starvation and disaster to decent standards of living, has been weakened by a combination of economic non-achievement and frightening population growth. On average, African women each give birth to six babies; Africa's inhabitants are supplemented each month by more than a million new mouths to feed.

During the first half of the 1980s – while food production in Asia and Latin America kept pace with population increases – the African continent's average economic growth slowed to 1.5 per cent a year. But during the same period, its population expanded so rapidly that income per person dropped annually by more than 1.5 per cent.

Development or underdevelopment?

Is colonialism to blame for the continent's present ills? The issue is whether colonialism promoted "development" or "underdevelopment." According to one school of thought, the results of European rule are generally held to be progressive.

Those who disagree argue that an African economic "takeoff" was hindered by the colonial experience. The European powers are said to have left the continent's economies in a position of permanent dependence on the West. While agreeing that most African countries underwent considerable economic growth after 1945, they say this led to growth without development. Dependence led to underdevelopment because it allowed African resources to be exploited rather than developed by Western interests even after independence. In short, economic neo-colonialism replaced political colonialism.

However, it seems clear that the weakness of the continent's development cannot very well be blamed entirely on the world's industrialized states (the West and the Eastern bloc), tempting though this explanation has been to many Africans themselves. There is a new recognition that African governments have made a major contribution to the disasters they face. To retain power at any price – rather than dealing with pressing economic problems – is all too often the primary objective of African regimes.

Overspending, wasting money on prestige projects, irresponsible borrowing from abroad, low output in the agricultural sector (where 80 per cent of Africans live and work), financial mismanagement and chronic corruption at all levels have all contributed to the continent's economic nightmare. These limitations have stretched the social and educational services of Africa to breaking point, constituting a serious development problem.

But by no means are all of Africa's troubles its own fault. The prices of its exports have fluctuated and fallen; more generally, the continent has felt the impact of a worldwide recession as well as the calamities of climatic and other natural diasters. Also, during the 1970s, the real price of oil increased fivefold, which was a blow for all non-petroleum producing countries. In Tanzania, for example, oil imports represented only 10 per cent of the value of exports in 1972 but by 1980 they had risen to 60 per cent.

It should also be said that, until recently at least, heavy government borrowing was not discouraged by commercial bankers and development agencies.

Today, the continent's overseas loans amount to $180 billion. Repayment is painfully high in proportion to the incomes of most African states. As a result, hospitals and clinics are desperately short of medicines and drugs, schools are in need of basic textbooks and factories close through lack of spare parts for machinery.

The political fallout

It is against this backdrop of escalating economic crisis that one must assess the continent's political problems. Independence triggered rising expectations. Early dreams have been overtaken by mounting frustration. One reason for this is that the past quarter century has witnessed a parallel process: a growing gap between the standards of life among urban and rural peoples, and between the rich and the poor. In Africa, more than two-thirds of the population live in conditions of extreme poverty. Their ranks are growing daily.

The inability to meet popular demands and contain the disruptive forces of regional, ethnic and religious antagonisms within their borders have set a pattern of political instability in the majority of African countries. This is seen in the long drawn-out guerrilla campaigns conducted by rebels whose support is based on the peoples of particular localities, secessionist wars, cross-border invasions over disputed frontiers, and armed confrontations between rival communities.

The Markhait relief camp in the Sudan, 1986.

Another striking characteristic of the political landscape has been competition between civilian and military elites and the emergence of soldiers as key actors in the business of government. Militarism, as seen in the high incidence of coups and countercoups and in rising defense budgets on armaments (for use against neighbors or to suppress internal unrest), has become an enduring feature of independent Africa. The intrusion of great-power rivalry into the continent's domestic affairs has added a further element of instability.

Successes

Yet for all the above, the record is not uniformly wretched. It would be a mistake to say the continent was a region of constant turmoil and disagreement. Some leaders such as Banda of Malawi and Houphouët-Boigny of Ivory Coast have been successful in establishing stable, orderly and relatively prosperous regimes. In addition, a handful of presidents (Senghor of Senegal, Ahmadu Ahidjo of Cameroun and Nyerere of Tanzania) have retired gracefully after more than two decades in office.

While the OAU has done little to prevent divisions between its members, it has achieved a common front on the issue of South Africa. Hatred of apartheid unites most Africans. Although South Africa does not have the bloodiest government on the continent (it is not Amin's Uganda or Mengistu's Ethiopia), its system of racial domination attracts almost universal condemnation.

A determination to topple the South African regime and loosen its grip on Namibia has proved a powerful rallying point for African unity. However, the chances of an early resolution to the conflict in the subcontinent appear negligible. A long war of attrition lies ahead in the south.

The search for solutions

There are both long-term and short-term perspectives to the solution of Africa's problems. But since poverty is itself destabilizing and a cause of war and civil strife, the highest priority must be given to realistic programs for development. Like charity, it is now argued, economic development must begin at home. This requires a slow-down in Africa's frantic population explosion and an emphasis on human resource development. There is a new appreciation of the need to reverse "top-down" development, where decisions are taken by outside governments or agencies.

Instead, "bottom-up" development is being stressed in which individual men and women are encouraged to work for basic needs at the local level.

Although Africa will continue to rely on foreign aid, the task is to see that it is applied in the most effective way. In the past, development has been stunted not by lack of money but by its misapplication, especially on industrial investment and military spending. Today, as the 1986 Oxfam *For Richer For Poorer* report concludes, there is a new understanding and awareness of Africa's economic plight.

If the poverty war is to be overcome, the emphasis must be on rural development and the attainment of food self-sufficiency. Thus, an agricultural revolution is necessary for economic progress and the key to political stability.

However, given the continent's history of upheaval, this is unlikely to happen very easily. Predictions about Africa's future suggest that conflict and instability will continue to threaten the majority of its peoples well into the 21st century. For a tenth of humanity, the prospects for peace and prosperity seem bleak.

Peasant farmer in Ethiopia. Only an agricultural revolution can stem the tide of hunger and poverty.

CONFLICT IN THE 20th CENTURY: APPENDICES

By the turn of the century, Africa had been carved up among the major European powers. Both the process of occupation and the speed of decolonization were hastened by the activities of charismatic personalities, many of whom left an indelible mark on the continent. Yet independence failed to bring peace and prosperity to the region.

PERSONALITIES

Idi Amin Dada (1925-) Ugandan dictator. Born in the Kakwa region, West Nile, he joined the King's African Rifles in 1946. Between 1951-60 he was heavyweight boxing champion of Uganda. By 1967 Amin was a brigadier in the Ugandan Army. He deposed the civilian prime minister, Milton Obote, in the 1971 military coup, making himself "Life President" in 1976. His tyrannical regime was overthrown in the Tanzanian invasion of 1979 and he fled to Libya. He now lives in exile in Jeddah, Saudi Arabia.

Benjamin Nnamdi Azikiwe (1904-) President of Nigeria. Of Ibo origin, he was born in Zungeru, Northern Nigeria. After graduating from universities in the United States, he returned to Africa in 1934 and became president of the National Council of Nigeria and the Cameroons (NCNC) in 1946. His Nigerian presidency lasted from 1963-66 when a military coup replaced him. He joined the rebel Biafra cause in 1967 but later sought reconciliation with the Federal government. In 1979 he unsuccessfully contested the presidential elections.

Kenneth Kaunda (1924-) President of Zambia. Born at Lubwa, he became a schoolteacher and a welfare officer. A leading African nationalist politician, he was elected first president of the United National Independence Party in 1960. When Zambian independence was achieved in October 1964, he became his country's first president, a post he still holds. An outspoken critic of apartheid, he chaired the Organization of African Unity during 1970-71.

Mobutu Sese Seko (1930-) President of Zaire. Born in what was then the Belgian Congo, he became involved in politics through the *Mouvement National Congolaise*. He was an army delegate at the Brussels Round Table conference on Congo independence, 1959-60. As Chief of Military Staff in 1960, he seized supreme power for a few months soon after independence. Five years later he deposed President Kasavubu in his second *coup d'état*. Dedicated to national unity, he has held his vast country together despite serious secessionist attempts.

Gamal Abdel Nasser (1918-1970) Egyptian political leader. The son of a post office worker, he graduated from the Cairo Military Academy in 1938. In 1948 he saw active service when Egyptian forces unsuccessfully invaded Israel. The same year Nasser formed the Free Officers' Committee which planned the reformist *coup d'état* of July 1952. He became prime minister in 1954 and president two years later. His political career survived the Egyptian defeat in the Arab-Israeli war of 1967 but he became increasingly dependent on Soviet military aid. He died in office in 1970.

Mobutu Sese Seko

Gamal Abdel Nasser

Kwame Nkrumah (1909-1972) President of Ghana. A former teacher who was educated in the United States and Britain, he was General Secretary of the West African National Secretariat in London (1945-47). In 1949 he formed the Convention People's Party, demanding "Self-Government Now." Imprisoned by the British colonial authorities for organizing illegal strikes in 1950, he became Ghana's first prime minister at independence in 1957 and president in 1960. His radical one-party regime was overthrown by an army-police coup in February 1966. Nkrumah died as an exile in Guinea.

Julius Nyerere (1922-) President of Tanzania. The son of a chief, Dr Nyerere was born near Lake Victoria in 1922. He was educated at Makerere College, Uganda, and Edinburgh University. The founder of the Tanganyika African National Union (TANU) in 1954, his presidency began with independence in 1964. In one of the few African examples of a peaceful transfer of power, he handed over his office to Ali Hassan Musinyi in 1985.

Nelson Mandela (1918-) South African Nationalist leader. The son of the Tembu tribe's chief, he was

Julius Nyerere

born in Transkei and educated as a lawyer at the University College of Fort Hare and at the Witwatersrand University. He was detained in 1956 as national organizer of the African National Congress. Having been tried for treason, he was acquitted in 1961 but rearrested the following year and sentenced to life imprisonment in June 1964. At present he is being held at Pollsmoor prison, near Cape Town.

Haile Selassie I (1892-1975) Emperor of Ethiopia. Born into a dynasty claiming descent from King Solomon and the Queen of Sheba, he became prince regent in 1916. He was crowned emperor after the death of Empress Zauditu in 1930. During 1967-70, he played a leading mediating role in the Nigerian civil war. Placed under house arrest by the new military government during the 1974 coup, he died in suspicious circumstances in 1975.

Léopold Sédar Senghor (1906-) President of Senegal and poet. Educated at the Lycée de Dakar in Senegal and the University of Paris, he was a schoolteacher in France from 1935-1948. A leading poet of the *négritude* movement, he was elected a Socialist Party deputy to the French National Assembly in 1945. Recognized as the elder

statesman of French-speaking Africa, he was president of Senegal from 1960 until his retirement in 1980.

Ian Smith (1919-) Prime Minister of Rhodesia. Educated at Rhodes University in South Africa, he served as a fighter pilot with the Royal Air Force during the Second World War. He was prime minister of Rhodesia between 1964-79, proclaiming the Unilateral Declaration of Independence from Britain in November 1965. Following the protracted guerrilla war against his government and the transfer to black majority rule in 1980, Smith became a Zimbabwean Opposition MP.

Hendrik Verwoerd (1901-1966) South African Prime Minister. Born in the Netherlands, he emigrated to South Africa as a child. Educated at the Universities of Hamburg, Leipzig and Berlin, he was appointed Professor of Applied Psychology at Stellenbosch University. In 1937 he became editor of the notoriously pro-Nazi newspaper *Die Transvaaler*. Closely associated with the early development of apartheid theory, he was able to put it into practice on becoming prime minister in 1958. He was assassinated in September 1966.

Nelson Mandela

Léopold Senghor

APARTHEID

In the years since 1945, the internal policies of South Africa have been subject to more controversy and criticism than those of virtually any other state. The reason for this is apartheid – the Afrikaans (the South African language derived from Dutch) word for apartness or separation. The term came into use in 1948 when it was the election slogan of the successful National Party which has ruled South Africa ever since. It means a system of racial laws ensuring white rule over the black majority.

Racial separation

However, the origins of apartheid predate the Union of South Africa (1910) and the 1948 election. Since the original white settlement of the Cape of Good Hope by the Dutch East India Company in 1652, relations between whites and sparsely scattered black communities were based on the dominant position of Europeans. During the following three centuries, segregation (separation) of the races spread as the major social pattern of white South Africa. What is peculiar about apartheid is that, in a period when colonialism and racial separation were everywhere on the retreat, South Africa was moving toward the total enforcement of segregation by law.

The legal system

Modern policies of territorial separation have their origin in the Bantu Land Act of 1913 (amended in 1936) which designates 13 per cent of the land to "natives" on African reserves. Although the black population makes up almost three-quarters of the population, most of the remaining 87 percent of the land is allocated to whites (16 percent of the population).

Also in 1936, the small number of blacks who did have the vote were removed from the same electoral register as whites and placed on a separate African voters' list. So began a process by which black and later Cape Coloreds (those of mixed race) were denied common political rights with whites. To the European minority, the principle of "one man, one vote" is unacceptable as it would destroy their hold on power.

From 1950 when the chief "architect of apartheid," Dr Hendrik Verwoerd, was appointed Minister of Native Affairs, laws tightened up the system. Petty apartheid describes a range of measures which separate races in their everyday activities. In the past, these included total segregation on transport and in shops, sport, entertainment, hotels, restaurants, beaches and in some churches.

Grand apartheid describes the more fundamental separation of political and economic activity. For

In 1986 whites-only buses were allowed to carry black people. This provoked a mixed response from white people.

many years, blacks were not allowed to strike or to belong to trade unions. A policy, known as Job Reservation, denied them access to skilled jobs. And the Group Areas Act of 1950 designated areas where blacks and whites were allowed to live.

Separate development

The Promotion of the Bantu Self-Government Act of 1959 provided the framework for the future development of "separate development." Ten self-governing *bantustans* or "homelands" for different African tribes were identified, where blacks (millions of whom were forcefully removed to these areas) would exercise their political rights. Four of these – Transkei, Bophuthatswana, Venda and Ciskei – have been given a form of legal independence. But the homelands are not recognized outside South Africa.

One reason for this is that they are not self-sufficient countries. Their peoples live in very poor conditions. At present they are home to half of South Africa's blacks. The other 12 million migrate to employment in white South Africa. Officially, the black residents of white South Africa are citizens of their tribal-based homeland.

Opposition to apartheid

Apartheid was opposed by large sections of the black population because it was racist and they wanted a political system based on black majority rule. The main black political organization was the illegal African National Congress. But in the past four decades, South Africa has used harsh security measures to crush opposition, for example, during the Soweto riots in 1976.

Reform

Although the South African regime is often thought to be unbending in its attitude to apartheid, the late 1970s and early 1980s witnessed some movement away from the rigid ideas of Dr Verwoerd. As President P. W. Botha put it, apartheid "must adapt or die." In the economic sphere, black trade unions (and in some industries, strikes) were legalized. Job Reservation was relaxed, as were the Pass Laws (which made it compulsory for blacks to carry a pass in order to move about the country). But an identity card was introduced that all – including whites – have to carry.

At a social level, some elements of petty apartheid were modified or abolished. Many shops and public buildings were desegregated, as were numerous hotels, restaurants and beaches. The highly symbolic Mixed Marriages and Immorality Acts, outlawing inter-racial marriage and prohibiting sexual relations across the color lines, were repealed. However, the crucially important Group Areas Act remains; so too does the Population Registration Act which provides for race classification.

The centerpiece of Botha's reform program was the new constitution, introduced in 1983 with a separate chamber each for the whites, coloreds and Asians. But there was no chamber for blacks. The result was an explosion of black outrage which ignited in the Vaal Triangle townships south of Johannesburg.

Since 1984, South Africa has experienced widespread political unrest and considerable bloodshed. The government responded by suspending its program of reform and declaring a national state of emergency. Whether apartheid's future will be dominated by evolution or revolution is as yet to be decided.

The first victim of the Soweto riots, 1976.

FAMINE IN AFRICA

In the wake of the worst continent-wide famine of the century, the increasing inability of most African states to meet the food needs of their people is well-established. At its height in 1985, the famine in Africa was affecting one-third of the entire population. Some 150 million people were short of food. Since independence, when Africa was able to feed itself, the population has increased by 3 per cent every year. But food production has increased by only half that rate. Much – but not all – of the resulting shortfall has been made up by importing foreign foodstuffs.

Economic problems

This tendency to import food would not be so serious but for the fact that the price of commodities such as coffee and copper has fallen in real terms by some 20 per cent in as many years. Since this is the main way of earning cash to pay for imports and development, Africans have found themselves caught in an international poverty trap from which they appear unable to extricate themselves.

Unfortunately, government policies often make the problem worse. Expensive show-piece projects soak up vast resources with little obvious benefit to most ordinary Africans. Glittering cities built in the image of the developed world do not lead to advances in African society. Where more practical attempts at development have been made, these have tended to favor complex industrial projects at the expense of peasant agriculture.

Agricultural chaos

To make matters worse, interstate conflicts and civil strife have added to the chaos. Political instability, together with government incompetence, must take a share of the blame for famine in the continent at large. These conditions do not encourage the settlement and cultivation of the land.

In many countries, the whole food-chain has been disrupted. Climatic catastrophes and wars combine to destroy farms and livestock. Frequently, people are afraid to go out into the fields. Those who continue to farm are desperately short of seed, hoes and irrigation equipment.

The other problem is that farmers in many instances have little incentive to produce more than they themselves need. This is because the transportation system may have been completely destroyed by rebels, and farmers cannot sell their produce at the usual markets.

Doctors from Europe tend the sick and hungry in a camp in Ethiopia, 1986.

be cataclysmic. Swarms of 40 billion locusts are feared capable of devouring 80,000 tons of crops each day – enough to provide food for almost half a million people for a year.

In 1984, television pictures of the Ethiopian camp at Korem revealed to the outside world the pitiful faces and emaciated bodies of starving families. But what could be done? Bob Geldof offered one powerful, no-nonsense answer. Impatient with officialdom, his idea of Band Aid/Live Aid concerts raised $75 million. Wisely spent, this money will make a valuable contribution to famine relief.

Long-term solutions

However, relieving the symptoms rather than tackling the underlying causes is only a short-term answer. International aid to avert famine will save people from dying for a few months but it does little to restore peasant agriculture. For this, African states need help with a long-term strategy aimed at preventing, rather than alleviating, famine. For example, the dumping of unwanted surpluses from developed countries may be doubly unhelpful – simultaneously creating a taste for expensive imported food while forcing down the prices of local produce. In these circumstances, local farmers cannot make a living.

Non-food aid can often be better suited to re-establishing peasant independence. But even here there are problems. The gift of a water-pump is not sufficient when its failure causes the season's crop to wither in the sun. Thus, the original act of generosity has to be backed by the mundane but equally vital supply of spare parts and training in maintenance techniques.

It is this kind of detailed and painstaking planning that will help Africa escape the ravages of famine by rebuilding itself on the solid foundations of traditional agricultural self-sufficiency. Ultimately, reform must be home-grown, not the "quick-fix" of imported instant aid.

Swarms of locusts destroyed many new crops in 1986.

Political problems

Currently there are major wars in Angola, Ethiopia, Western Sahara, Mozambique, Chad and Sudan. In the last three of these, the conflicts have severely disrupted agricultural production, causing massive population movements as peasants abandon their plots and move to the relative safety of the towns. In Ethiopia, food has become a political weapon to reach and control the people. The pro-Soviet ruling military junta has forcibly resettled millions of peasants in an attempt to cut off support to guerrillas. One agency, *Médecins sans Frontières* (Doctors without Frontiers), calculated that by 1986 up to 100,000 had died through this policy of "villagization." Of the eight million Ethiopians now believed to be critically short of food, a million will probably die.

Sometimes, regimes at war with their own people have hampered the work of relief organizations. One United Nations' effort (Operation Rainbow) to fly food into war-torn southern Sudan in 1986, where two million famine-struck people live, was threatened by the government's refusal to guarantee safe passage for aircraft moving emergency supplies into rebel-controlled territory. In 1985, the Ethiopian government nearly rejected a British Royal Air Force relief operation, claiming it was a Western attempt to undermine the regime.

Drought

Drought, along with the diseases that follow in its wake, has played a central role in the famine. And the rains that promise relief from famine sometimes lead to flooding and locusts. In the most serious infestation for 60 years, a locust plague of unprecedented proportions began swarming across vast areas of the African continent in 1986, destroying precious food crops in its path. The consequences can

FOREIGN INTERVENTION

Foreign intervention means the deployment of non-African forces (sometimes in collaboration with an African state) from *outside* the continent. These interventions can be designed either to support or to oppose the governments of African states. The two superpowers (the United States and Soviet Union), together with Britain and France, have been the most active in this sphere, but other countries have also been involved.

In most cases, armed interventions have been bilateral, usually involving troop movements from just one country into another one. However, on a number of occasions, military intervention has been multilateral, involving several states sending expeditionary forces to impose peace throughout a particular territory.

Intervention in the Congo

The most famous example was the United Nations' intervention in the Congo civil war (1960-64). During that period, a total of 93,000 men from three dozen member countries – including several African ones – served at one time or another in the Congo. It met with considerable military success in preventing the secession of Katanga and in restoring order to the state.

The presence of mercenaries, yet another form of foreign intervention, has also affected the outcome of African conflicts – as in the Congo, Nigeria and the Sudan. In the Congo, for example, Tshombe believed that mercenaries were the answer to his secessionist dreams in 1960. When he came to power in 1964 as leader of a reunited state, he again hired mercenaries (under the command of a South African "soldier of fortune," Major Mike Hoare) – this time to defeat fresh secessionist threats.

Superpower rivalry

Rivalry in Africa has been enhanced by confrontation between the superpowers and their respective allies. The parties to this conflict have challenged – and threatened – each other for political influence, trade and military bases. With its three vital strategic seaways (Suez, the Horn and the Cape) and rich mineral wealth, the continent is a natural target for outside attention. In response, African governments have attempted to turn such involvement to their advantage (usually for their own domestic security), playing off one power against another.

France

It is France, rather than the superpowers, that has consistently played the most interventionist role in Africa. French influence is based on 20 former colonies and extends to the former Belgian territory of Zaire. Almost all the French-speaking countries have defense agreements with Paris and there are French garrisons in the Central African Republic, Djibouti, Gabon, Ivory Coast and Senegal. Most of the 7,500 troops are from the Marines or the *Légion Etrangère* (Foreign Legion).

The remarkable French record has included frequent interventions to restore order and to rescue African presidents from revolts and *coups d'état*: Congo-Brazzaville and Cameroun (1960), Mauritania (1961), Gabon (1962 and 1964), Niger (1963) and Chad (1970-79 and since 1983). The French also led the suppression

Foreign intervention in Africa in 1987

- Soviet and/or Cuban-assisted countries
- Countries subjected to French intervention
- United States-assisted countries

of the Shaba rebellions in Zaire of 1977 and 1978. The purpose of these actions was to guard the flow of minerals to Western countries and to protect Europeans, 200 of whom were massacred at Kolwezi in 1978.

In Operation Barracuda, President Giscard d'Estaing sent 650 paratroopers to the Central African Republic in 1979 to overthrow Bokassa and reinstall ex-President Dacko, whom Bokassa had overthrown with French help 13 years before. A sadistic murderer who had personally taken part in the killings of some 100 schoolchildren, Bokassa had become an embarrassment to the French. Unlike other European powers, therefore, France (often called the policeman of Africa) has never regarded decolonization as a retreat.

Great Britain

Of all the British interventions, the Suez episode was the shortest. On November 5, 1956, an assault force of 1,100 British and French paratroopers was dropped near Port Said in Egypt. The Suez Crisis was brought to a humiliating end in the face of confused political aims and worldwide criticism at Anglo-French "gunboat diplomacy."

During the Nigerian civil war (1967-70), however, the British and French supported opposing sides. Nevertheless, with the other major exception of armed intervention by invitation in 1964 – when British troops quickly put down army mutinies and restored law and order in Kenya, Tanganyika and Uganda – the United Kingdom has chosen not to become actively involved in African conflicts.

Soviet Union

While it has no historic ties with Africa, the Soviet Union is the only other power to match French military activities on the continent. Because it has adequate mineral reserves, the Soviet Union's main interest is strategic, especially on the Horn which is much more important to it than any other part of Africa. Therefore it gives massive support to Colonel Mengistu's Marxist regime in Ethiopia.

Overall, the Soviet Union has been most successful supporting national liberation movements in anti-colonial conflicts, for instance, FRELIMO in Mozambique. Today, the Soviet Union has also become the continent's main arms supplier.

Cuba

It is impossible to discuss Soviet efforts to reduce Western (and Chinese) influence without mentioning the decisive military impact of its principal agent, Cuba. In both the socialist states of Angola and Ethiopia, the regimes have been maintained largely thanks to the presence of Cuban troops. Their role can be partly explained by the Cuban leader Fidel Castro's words: "African blood," he said, "flows in our veins."

The United States

Although American involvement in Africa has grown since the mid-1970s, US influence has always remained piecemeal compared to its military interests elsewhere in the Third World. However, it has invested considerable military resources in Africa's two largest countries, the Sudan and Zaire, as well as in the strategically-located states of Kenya and Somalia.

In all four pro-West territories, United States interests have been furthered by large-scale military aid rather than through overt military involvement. But as with KGB (Soviet spying organization) clandestine operations on the continent, there can be little doubt of covert activity by the American Central Intelligence Agency.

Other countries

Other states whose activities deserve mention include Israel, whose rescue operation at Entebbe in 1976 demonstrated the ease with which a small but developed outsider could intervene in an African state; Belgium, which intervened twice with the French in Zaire; China, which has provided arms to liberation movements in an attempt to counter Soviet influence; and a number of East European states, who have supported Moscow.

French Legionnaires guard prisoners in northern Chad.

RHODESIAN COUNTERINSURGENCY

The insurgency against the Rhodesian government, 1966-79, can be divided into three phases. During the first phase, which began in early 1966, a series of armed clashes occurred in the Zambezi Valley. The Zimbabwe African National Union (ZANU) and Zimbabwe African People's Union (ZAPU) – the latter in conjunction with the African National Congress – infiltrated teams of insurgents across the Zambezi River from Zambia. The second phase saw the scene of fighting shift to northeastern Rhodesia, where ZANU launched a new offensive during the early 1970s from bases in FRELIMO-dominated areas of neighboring Mozambique.

During the third phase, which began after the collapse of Portuguese rule in Mozambique and the failure of the Victoria Falls Conference, the insurgency gradually spread across the entire country. ZANU extended its operations throughout eastern Rhodesia from bases in Mozambique, and ZAPU rather later in the day infiltrated western Rhodesia from bases in Botswana and Zambia. The insurgency thus evolved from periodic guerrilla incursions across the Zambezi into a sustained, nationwide conflict, and the Rhodesian authorities had to intensify their counterinsurgency campaign in accordance with the rising threat.

The first phase
During the opening round of the conflict, the Rhodesians responded to ZANU and ZAPU incursions into the Zambezi Valley by launching what were usually referred to as "search and destroy" operations, based upon information provided by reconnaissance teams and friendly African tribesmen. This tactic proved highly effective.

The Rhodesians were able to locate and eliminate virtually all the incoming guerrilla bands without straining their slender military resources, though their manpower was boosted from 1967 by the presence of South African paramilitary policemen, who stayed on in some strength until 1975.

The second phase
The Rhodesians adopted the same tactic at the outset of the insurgents' next offensive, launched by ZANU in northeastern Rhodesia in December 1972. This time, however, the security forces found it much more difficult to "find and fix" the guerrillas, particularly as the local tribesmen supported ZANU and were reluctant to provide information to the government side.

Rhodesian troops patrol the border areas in search of guerrillas, 1976.

As a result, the government had to authorize additional measures. These included the removal of a certain number of villagers into Protected Villages (PVs) to reduce the guerrillas' influence. Also a minefield barrier was laid down along parts of the border with Mozambique, to reduce guerrilla infiltration. In addition, "hot pursuit" raids were launched into Mozambican territory.

This counterinsurgency effort placed an increased burden on government forces, but it did enable the authorities gradually to reduce the ZANU threat. By the end of 1974 the security forces had accounted for over 500 ZANU guerrillas, and claimed to be well on the way to wiping out the last surviving guerrilla bands.

The third phase

Not surprisingly, therefore, the white Rhodesians responded to the escalation of the war, from early 1976 onwards, by using the same tactics but in an extended or refined form. As before, they concentrated on trying to attack the guerrillas, developing a technique known as "Fire Force." Small formations of airmobile crack troops, backed by helicopter gunships and armed Lynx aircraft, rushed off to intercept guerrillas spotted by ground reconnaissance teams.

The Rhodesians also persevered with the PV program as well as the minefield barrier, extending the latter to 864 km (540 miles) along the borders with Mozambique and Botswana. Moreover, they stepped up their cross-border operations, launching not just "hot pursuit" missions but also a whole series of devastating preemptive attacks on guerrilla bases in Mozambique, Zambia, Botswana and even Angola. These attacks were supplemented later in the war by strikes against economic targets in Mozambique and Zambia, designed to make the target states think twice about hosting the insurgents.

The third phase of the war also saw a key innovation by the Rhodesian government. In an attempt to deflect international pressure and undermine the insurgent movements, the authorities devised and implemented the so-called internal settlement, allowing for one-man one-vote elections and a black prime minister.

A military stalemate

This counterinsurgency campaign was in some respects highly effective. Certainly the Rhodesian security forces inflicted enormous casualties on the guerrillas, particularly during Fire Force operations and cross-border raids, at comparatively little cost to themselves. In military terms, indeed, the Rhodesians did remarkably well, considering their lack of sufficient manpower – even toward the end of the war the security forces fielded on average only 25,000 men – and their supply of equipment was hardly lavish.

For all that, however, the Rhodesians were unable to achieve more than a military stalemate. For one thing, they faced the grave disadvantage of being exposed to infiltration from three of their four neighbors. But the crucial disadvantage was in manpower. Even after tapping every conceivable source of white manpower and recruiting a substantial number of foreigners and Africans, the Rhodesians lacked the strength to defeat the insurgents. The latter were able to make good their losses to the extent that their armed strength numbered 10,000 by the war's end.

Nationalist victory

In fact as the war dragged on the government's human and economic resources were stretched to near breaking point, with the result that it had little choice but to accept the settlement terms offered by the British. By that time, of course, the insurgents too – or more accurately their principal hosts, Mozambique and Zambia – were eager for peace. They were able to win the last crucial battle: the British-sponsored elections. The fact that ZANU and ZAPU won a resounding victory in the elections demonstrated the fundamental flaw in Rhodesian counterinsurgency – that the authorities did not do nearly enough to win over the "hearts and minds" of the African population.

Airmobile troops run toward an Alouette helicopter, 1976.

CHRONOLOGY

1884-85

The Berlin Conference agrees a framework for the Partition of Africa

1899-1902

War in South Africa between the Boers and British forces

1910

May 31 South Africa achieves "Dominion" (independent) status

1922

February 28 Egypt gains internal self-government

1923

October 1 Britain hands over power in Southern Rhodesia to local white settler community

1948

May 26 Afrikaner National Party wins election in South Africa and begins to implement *apartheid*

1951

December 24 Independence of Libya

1952

July 23 Officers led by General Neguib and Colonel Nasser depose King Farouk of Egypt

September 11 Federation of Eritrea and Ethiopia

October 20 State of Emergency declared to counter Mau Mau threat in Kenya

1954

November 1 Outbreak of Algerian War of Independence

1956

January 1 Independence of the Sudan

March 2 Independence of Morocco

March 20 Independence of Tunisia

November 5 Anglo-French forces invade Egypt

1957

January-October Battle of Algiers; French paras crush FLN

March 6 Independence of Ghana

1958

May French troops in Algeria force change of government in Paris; de Gaulle comes to power

October 2 Independence of Guinea

November 17 General Abboud seizes power in the Sudan

1960

"The Year of Independence":
January 1 Cameroun
March 21 South African police kill 67 people at Sharpeville
April 27 Togo
June 20 Mali and Senegal
June 26 Madagascar
June 30 Belgian Congo (Zaire)
July 1 Somalia
July 5 Army mutiny in Belgian Congo sparks off civil war lasting until 1964.

August 1 Dahomey (Benin)
August 3 Niger
August 5 Upper Volta (Burkina Faso)
August 7 Ivory Coast
August 11 Chad
August 13 Central African Republic
August 15 Congo-Brazzaville
August 17 Gabon
October 1 Nigeria
November 28 Mauritania

1961

April 21 Attempted coup by French forces in Algeria

April 27 Independence of Sierra Leone

May 31 South Africa becomes a republic outside the Commonwealth

December 9 Independence of Tanganyika (name changed to Tanzania following union with Zanzibar on April 27, 1964)

1962

July 1 Independence of Burundi and Rwanda

July 3 Independence of Algeria

October 9 Independence of Uganda

1963

January 13 President Olympio of Togo assassinated

May 26 Organization of African Unity formed

December 10 Independence of Zanzibar

December 12 Federation of Central Africa dissolved; Independence of Kenya

1964

January 19-23   Army mutinies in Kenya, Tanganyika and Uganda put down with British assistance

July 6   Independence of Nyasaland (Malawi)

October 24   Independence of Northern Rhodesia (Zambia)

1965

February 18   Independence of The Gambia

June 19   President Ben Bella of Algeria ousted in coup d'état

November 11   Rhodesian settlers rebel against Britain and declare Unilateral Independence (UDI)

November 25   General Mobutu of Zaire seizes power in bloodless coup

1966

January 1   Colonel Bokassa seizes power in Central African Republic

January 15   Nigeria's first military coup

February 24   The first of Ghana's five coups d'état

September 30   Independence of Botswana

October 4   Independence of Lesotho

1967

May 31   Nigeria's Eastern Region (Biafra) secedes, leading to 2½-year civil war

1968

March 12   Independence of Mauritius

September 6   Independence of Swaziland

October 12   Independence of Equatorial Guinea

1969

Disastrous drought in countries of the Sahel lasts until 1974

September 1   Gaddafi's coup against King Idris of Libya

October 21   General Barre stages coup d'état in Somalia

1971

January 25   General Amin seizes power in Uganda

1974

April 25   Coup in Lisbon overthrows Caetano, paving the way for the collapse of Portugal's African empire

September 10   Independence of Guinea-Bissau

September 12   Coup dethrones Ethiopia's Emperor Haile Selassie

1975

February 28   Independence of Western Sahara

June 25   Independence of Mozambique

July 5   Independence of Cape Verde

July 6   Independence of Comoros

July 12   Independence of São Tomé et Principe

November 11   Independence of Angola; civil war breaks out (which continues following the MPLA victory, November 1976)

1976

June 16   Mass protests in South Africa's large black townships last until October 19, 1977

June 26   Independence of Seychelles

1977

June 27   Independence of Djibouti

July   Somalia invades Ogaden region of Ethiopia (forced to withdraw by March 1978)

1979

February   Tanzanian invasion of Uganda

1980

April 18   Independence of Zimbabwe

1981

October 6   President Sadat of Egypt assassinated

1982

January 1   Union of The Gambia and Senegal as Confederation of Senegambia

1984

March 18   Nkomati agreement between South Africa and Mozambique

1985

Drought in the Horn of Africa and Southern Africa lasts until 1986

April 1   President Nimeiri of the Sudan ousted in military coup

July 27   President Obote of Uganda ousted in military coup

December   Border clashes between Mali and Burkina Faso

1986

June 12   Nationwide State of Emergency declared by President Botha of South Africa

INDEX

Note: Numbers in bold refer to illustrations or maps

FURTHER READING

Achebe, C., *Things Fall Apart* (Fawcett, 1978).

Austin, D., *Politics in Africa*, 2nd ed. (Hanover, NH: University Press of New England, 1984).

Baynham, S. J., *Military Power and Politics in Black Africa* (St Martin, 1986).

Calvocoressi, P., *Independent Africa and the World* (Longman, 1985).

Cartwright, J., *Political Leadership in Africa* (St Martin, 1983).

Chaliand, G., *The Struggle for Africa: Politics of the Great Powers* (St Martin, 1982).

Davenport, T. R. H., *South Africa: A Modern History* (Buffalo, NY: Univ of Toronto Press, 1977).

Europa, *Africa South of the Sahara* (Lanham, MD: Unipub, annual).

First, R., *Libya: The Elusive Revolution* (Holmes & Meier, 1975).

Fage, J. & Oliver, R., *A Short History of Africa* (Knopf, 1979).

Gavshon, A., *Crisis in Africa: Battleground of East and West* (Penguin, 1981).

Griffiths, I. L. L., *An Atlas of African Affairs* (Methuen, 1984).

Hatch, J., *A History of Postwar Africa* (Methuen, 1967).

Legum, C. (ed), *Africa Contemporary Record* (Holmes & Meier, annual).

Mackenzie, J. M., *The Partition of Africa* (Methuen, 1983).

Martin, D. and Johnson, P., *The Struggle for Zimbabwe* (Winchester, MA: Faber & Faber, 1981).

Mazrui, A. A. & Tidy, M., *The Africans: A Triple Heritage* (Boston, MA: Little Brown, 1986).

Meredith, M., *The First Dance of Freedom: Black Africa in the Postwar Era* (Harper and Row, 1985).

Olaniyan, R., *Nigerian History and Culture*, Longman, 1984.

Oliver, R. & Crowder, M. (eds), *The Cambridge Encyclopedia of Africa* (Cambridge University Press, 1981).

Tordoff, W., *Government and Politics in Africa* (Bloomington, IN: Indiana University Press, 1985).

Wolfers, M., *Politics in the Organisation of African Unity* (Methuen, 1976)

(NOTE: All publishers located in New York unless specified otherwise.)

ACKNOWLEDGMENTS

Photographic Credits:
Cover: Frank Spooner Agency; page 5: Hutchison Library; page 8: Mary Evans Library; page 9: Malcolm Smythe; page 10: BBC Hulton; page 12: Mary Evans; page 14: Topham; page 15: Popperfoto; page 17: BBC Hulton; page 18: BBC Hulton; page 21: Popperfoto; page 22: Rex Features; page 24: Photosource/Keystone; page 25: Topham; page 27: Popperfoto; page 29: Popperfoto; page 30: The Research House; page 33: Popperfoto; page 35 (top): Rex Features; page 35 (bottom): Popperfoto; page 38: Network; page 39: Mike Goldwater/Network; page 41: Frank Spooner; page 43 (top): Stern; page 43: (bottom): Topham; page 44: Format; page 46: Format; page 47: Mike Goldwater/ Network; page 48 (both): Popperfoto; page 49 (top and center): Popperfoto; page 49 (bottom): BBC/Bettman Archives; page 50: Popperfoto; page 51: International Defense and Aid Fund for Southern Africa; page 52: Stern; page 56: The Research House; page 57: Frank Spooner.

The author would like to thank Nina Baynham, James Higgs, Matt Midlane and Francis Toase for their research assistance.